# It all begins with Insights.

Dr. Craig West

A QUICK GUIDE TO MAXIMIZING
THE VALUE OF YOUR BUSINESS

**Capitaliz**
BY SUCCESSION+

Dr. Craig West
Succession Plus Pty Ltd
Level 6, 50 York St
SYDNEY NSW 2000
www.succession.plus

Author Services: https://www.pickawoowoo.com/

First published in 2023.

A catalogue record for this book is available from the National Library of Australia.

ISBN: 9780992293932
ISBN: 9782992293925 (eBook)

# CONTENTS

It all
begins
with
Insights.

# Introduction

As an accountant from a public practice background and a strategic business advisor, I've been helping businesses grow and prepare for exit for over 20 years.

What I found, is there are a lot of businesses that make bad exits, either failing completely or exiting with bad outcomes, wrong pricing, wrong structure, or having paid too much tax et cetera. There are also several businesses that were badly prepared, or simply not prepared at all for their exit. That led me to realize my passion for finding out why this status quo is the most likely outcome for so many business owners - and doing something about it.

Since 2009, my boutique advisory practice, Succession Plus, has been helping mid-market business owners design and implement a business succession and exit plan to maximize sale value upon exit. Our practice is the largest consulting practice specifically focused on succession and exit planning in Australia, New Zealand, and the United Kingdom.

I am passionate about Business Succession and Exit Planning and the difference it can make for owners and economies. The wealth tied up in privately owned businesses internationally is tens of trillions of dollars. Having worked with over 800 clients over 12 years and seen very few other effective models I decided to digitize our learnings and build a system advisors could use worldwide to help business owners maximize the value of their business and achieve a successful exit. CAPITALIZ was created.

Capitaliz aims to capture all the intellectual property, experience (including mistakes), and learnings we made in building Succession Plus and working with clients.

You can't just start to think about it when you turn 64. If you don't plan, you get a poor price. But a good exit plan is a win-win-win for everyone - you get the best price, the buyer gets a good business, and your customers and staff are looked after.

At Succession Plus we take a holistic view of succession planning, looking at your business and personal goals and putting processes and systems in place to help you reach the best outcome, offering expert advice in management, taxation, employee incentives and accounting issues.

We've identified several steps that you can take to dramatically improve the performance and preparedness of your business, and hence the value on exit. We take you through those steps over a few years as you go through the gradual stages of transition.

It All Begins with Insights – understanding exactly what your privately owned business looks like, what it is worth and what exit options are available and what needs to be done to identify, protect, maximize, and extract your value. At the heart of Capitaliz, is the **Business Insights Report** - a comprehensive evaluation and guide as to what needs to be done to maximize the value of the business and achieve a successful exit.

## Dr. Craig West
Founder & Chairman, Succession Plus

# Prologue

*"If you want to build a business you can sell for maximum value, Craig West is the best in the field. Whether it's through his books, courses, or advisory programs, if you can get in front of him, do it."*

Jack Delosa - Executive Director of The Entourage and MBE Education

*"Exit planning should be part of every business owner's strategic business plan. We should always be prepared to get hit by that proverbial truck.*

*Don't put off establishing your exit plan till tomorrow. Start today to maximize the value of your life on this earth by reading this book."*

Peter G. Christman, CEPA - The Original Exit Planning Coach and Mentor; CEO, The Christman Group - Value Enhancement

*"Exiting is not the end; it's the beginning of your next life. Plan for what you are going to do after the exit and make sure you have discussed the plan with trusted advisors, family, and friends. If you are not prepared, choose to take the next year or two to get prepared or risk ending up in the category of those who regret selling. Capitaliz will help you to choose your time and maximize your results on exit."*

Christopher M. Snider, CEPA - CEO of the Exit Planning Institute and Author of Walking to Destiny

# What is business succession and exit planning all about?

Most people go into business not only to earn an annual income but, more importantly, to ultimately extract the wealth created with a lump sum to fund their retirement or next venture. But many don't think about how to exit their business until it's nearly time to retire. Worse, many find they are forced to sell or leave their business suddenly due to illness, disability, debt, bankruptcy, legal disputes, or divorce.

You can't just put up a 'for sale' price on your business and expect that someone will come along and pay you the price you want. And if you decide to put an advertisement in the paper or online, don't think that the price you get represents the true value of your business.

For business owners, the business may be the largest asset with the family home coming second. Yet many business owners will spend more time and effort preparing the family home for sale than their business.

Most of us wouldn't just do a quick tidy up two weeks before the auction of our home and hope for the best. Selling a business, just like starting a business, requires a strategic plan, whether you plan to sell to family, employees, or complete strangers. Otherwise, you risk losing the long-term value of the investment that you have worked hard to create.

Understanding the three key factors of Business Succession and Exit Planning is critical to developing a successful plan. The co-ordination and preparation of the three factors is what ultimately leads to a successful exit.

The Business - Most businesses are not exit or sale ready, they are owner dependent and often lack effective systems and processes. Even though some of them can be quite large, they, may still be run like small businesses.

**The Owner/s** - Most baby boomer business owners are very strongly "attached" to their business. They identify with the business in what is called role-identity fusion. They need time and space to get comfortable about what their exit looks like and importantly, what life after the business means.

**The Money** - The business, the owner/s and their finances are often complicated and interwoven and therefore hard to separate. The Exit Planning Institute estimates that up to 90% of an owner's wealth is tied up in and linked to the business.

A strategic succession plan is a vision of the future, broken into the steps you need to take to achieve that vision. To maximize the value of your business on exit, you must plan your exit long before it happens. This will allow you time for a smooth transition, but it will also give you much better security should anything unexpected happen to you, the other shareholders, or your family members.

Business Succession Planning is a holistic process designed to help you align your personal and financial goals with your business performance and value. We help you to identify the current position and value of your business; the price you need for your business sale to meet your personal objectives and then develop a strategy to help you bridge the gap.

The process from planning to exit may need three to five years. Our aim is to have your business adequately prepared and at peak performance to ensure you get the best return. If you are passing the business on to family members, we help you put processes in place to make sure the business doesn't crumble the minute you hang up your keys. We will explain to you that **WHO** buys your business is a key factor in the price that you achieve and help you to position your business so that you can attract the best buyer.

The most successful business succession plans are those that have been carefully and slowly considered over a period, are implemented gradually, constantly monitored and reviewed, have realistic strategic outcomes, and **"Begin with the end in mind"**.

# The 21- Step Process

We use and recommend a five-stage process, each stage focused around identifying, protecting, maximizing, extracting, and managing business value. Each of these stages have several key steps, 21 in all, designed to effectively prepare the business, the owner and the financial position to maximize business value and achieve a successful exit.

This process has been developed over time. When I first published Enjoy It in 2006, our process had only 9 steps mainly focused on preparing the business, however as we worked with clients and learned more about their needs and the issues that were stopping them from becoming successful, the process was further developed into 11, then 15, and finally 21 steps. The process now covers all the key issues: business, personal, and financial to ensure maximum success.

The process allows time and space for owners to become very clear on what Business Succession and Exit Planning means to them. For many it is not about the money - more about preserving their legacy, looking after staff, customers, and suppliers. As such the process needs to identify the key drivers and aspirations of the founders and secondly, provide a mechanism for them to be successful in achieving those key goals and outcomes.

To fully implement the 21 steps, we typically work with clients over a 12 to18-month period (and with some clients significantly longer) and we always work closely with the clients' key advisors - accountant, financial planner, lawyers, bankers, and the like. This will help speed up the process and ensure the best possible result. This is very much a trusted advisor relationship model, and we work closely with the owners, family members, key employees, and other stakeholders to balance interest and ensure all business succession and exit planning needs are met.

We use our 21-step process to exiting your business over five stages with all clients:

- Stage One:      **Identify Value**
- Stage Two:      **Protect Value**
- Stage Three:   **Maximize Value**
- Stage Four:     **Extract Value**
- Stage Five:     **Manage Value**

## The 21-Step Business Succession and Exit Planning Process

| BUSINESS SUCCESSION AND EXIT PLAN | | | |
|---|---|---|---|
| | **Stage One:** Identify Value | STEP 1: | Goals and Outcomes |
| | | Step 2: | Fact Find |
| | | Step 3: | Business Insights Report |
| | **Stage Two:** Protect Value | Step 4: | Financial Planning |
| | | Step 5: | Unplanned Events |
| | | Step 6: | De-risking |
| | **Stage Three:** Maximize Value | Step 7: | Exit Options |
| | | Step 8: | Strategic Planning Business Model |
| | | Step 9: | Strategic Financials |
| | | Step 10: | Systems and Procedures |
| | | Step 11: | Marketing and Sales |
| | | Step 12: | Corporate Governance |
| | | Step 13: | Ownership Mindset |
| | | Step 14: | Employee Ownership |
| | | Step 15: | Management Succession |
| | **Stage Four:** Extract Value | Step 16: | Tax Planning |
| | | Step 17: | Documentation |
| | | Step 18: | Liquidity Event |
| | **Stage Five:** Manage Value | Step 19: | Ongoing Investment Planning |
| | | Step 20: | Asset Protection |
| | | Step 21: | Estate Planning |

The M3 Framework by OrangeKiwi (orangekiwillc.com) has three headings, as you can see in the illustration - **My Business**, **My Money**, and **My Self** - with eight boxes surrounding them. These are the issues that build the business. This closely aligns with the Exit Planning Institute model of business, finances (both business and owners) and personal (life after business) all being prepared for a succession or exit event.

## Why is now a good time to think about business succession and exit planning?

As any financial planner will tell you, the average amount needed to fund retirement in Australia is at least $1 million. We are living longer than ever before, and life expectancy is constantly improving, so we need more money to fund retirement, unless of course we wish to rely on a government pension. An Australian male who is 50 years old in 2021 can expect to live until 82 years old and females to 86 years. That's potentially around 20 years to fund in retirement.

Number (in thousands)

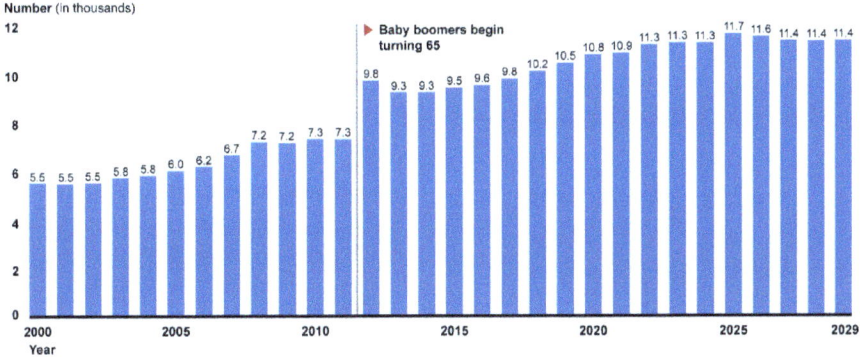

Source: GAO analysis of U.S. Census Bureau information. | GAO-17-579T

The baby boomer generation began turning 65 in 2011, and from now until 2030 over 10,000 Americans will hit retirement age each day. Interestingly, they own 60% of small businesses employing approximately 60.6 million employees, and over half of these baby boomer business owners have not only failed to complete a succession plan, but many have also not even considered preparing one.

In Australia, it is estimated that over the next decade the retirement of family business owners will see the transfer of approximately $1.6 trillion in wealth, which surely must make succession planning one of the most significant issues facing small to medium enterprise (SME) owners. In the United States this number is closer to $10 trillion.

Yet incredibly, despite 61% of business owners surveyed admitting their businesses are not sale or succession ready, 52.2% do not intend to do anything about it over the next twelve months.

## Business Exits

The Australian Bureau of Statistics reports that as of June 30, 2021, there are 2,402,254 actively trading businesses in the Australian economy.

In 2020-21, there was a:

- 3.8%, or 87,806, increase in the number of businesses
- 15.8% entry rate, with 365,480 entries
- 12.0% exit rate, with 277,674 exits.

| Year | Entries | Exits | Net change |
|---|---|---|---|
| 2017-18 | 343,888 | 273,237 | 70,651 |
| 2018-19 | 346,946 | 286,395 | 60,551 |
| 2019-20 | 336,499 | 291,049 | 45,450 |
| 2020-21 | 365,480 | 277,674 | 87,806 |

Source: Australian Bureau of Statistics, Counts of Australian Businesses, including Entries and Exits July 2017 – June 2021

Based on the most recently released United States Census Bureau (Feb 2022), the number of businesses in the USA is:

| | Firms | Employment | Annual payroll (000's) |
|---|---|---|---|
| 01: Total | 6,102,412 | 132,989,428 | $7,428,553,593 |
| 02: <5 employees | 3,777,085 | 6,003,770 | $294,917,415 |
| 03: 5-9 employees | 1,013,629 | 6,681,959 | $267,500,052 |
| 04: 10-19 employees | 640,827 | 8,632,696 | $358,971,177 |
| 05: <20 employees | 5,431,541 | 21,318,425 | $921,388,644 |
| 06: 20-99 employees | 555,046 | 21,762,863 | $995,870,795 |
| 07: 100-499 employees | 94,957 | 18,612,620 | $1,008,135,146 |
| 08: <500 employees | 6,081,544 | 61,693,908 | $2,925,394,585 |
| 09: 500+ employees | 20,868 | 71,295,520 | $4,503,159,008 |

Approx. 8.5% percent have been exiting each year (just over 2 million) – this number is low and often does not include family succession and transitions.

As a responsible business owner, it makes sense to start your exit strategy when you are 'at your peak' - ideally when the business is doing well, and you have the energy and enthusiasm to make the appropriate changes. Many business owners are finding it hard to keep up with technology and the new competitive environment that it brings. If you feel defeated and lose market share your business value will diminish, so start the process when you still have some fight and passion for your business. You may need to grow your business to make it more attractive to a buyer, or you may need to transition client relationships gradually to other key people within the business.

In the current market the best chance of success is to be prepared and plan. If you always "Begin with the end in mind", you are much better prepared with the right information for making the right decisions along the way and following the steps towards your long-term vision. If you start preparation early, you will get a deeper understanding of the potential value of your business and have the time available to you to make the changes required to increase your chances of a good exit.

On a financial level, a well-planned business exit will not only enable you to attract a higher sell price, but it will also let you minimize tax on the proceeds, using staged payments, superannuation contributions and taking full advantage of tax concessions. If you put your business up for sale suddenly, you may be met with a tax bill just when you don't need it.

Finally, if you do have to exit from your business unexpectedly due to poor health or other issues, the further you are down your exit plan, the better the outcome is likely to be for you and your family.

As business owners approach retirement, most will cease to own their businesses, however, up to 83% have no defined or documented business succession or exit plan. The KPMG report on family business states that 76% of family businesses intend to appoint a new CEO in the next five years and further that 72% expect to have some transfer of ownership in the next five years. This represents a large number of transitions over the next ten years and a large amount of wealth to be "transferred". The transfer of ownership represents a significant stage in entrepreneurial activity. It is through this transition that the founders remove themselves from the business they own. This relates to ownership, decision making and generating a capital surplus for their efforts.

## Identifying Value

I am going to take you through the first stage of our unique 21-step process designed specifically to help you to reach a successful business exit. This is not a do-it-yourself process; you will need to get some help and advice along the way. The better you understand the process, the more you can get involved, take on the tasks that you can do, and have clear expectations of the people who advise you on the rest. In the introduction I've focused on why planning is important, and consistent with that, I'll go through the initial steps, in the **Identifying Value** stage in more detail. Once you are clear about where you are trying to head and why, getting there is a whole lot easier.

Importantly, EVERY SINGLE ONE of the 800 clients we have worked with since 2009 has gone through this initial stage and ALL have used a Business Insights Report to understand exactly where they are at and what needs to be done.

# Case Study

The following case study will take you through each step of the five stages to exiting your business. The material includes the intellectual property of Succession Plus Pty Ltd who claims copyright ownership, including the detailed explanation of the 21-Step Business Succession and Exit Planning process, tools and templates used in our Capitaliz software platform to deliver that process to business owners.

This material must not be reproduced or distributed without the express written permission of the owner.

## Background

Mr. & Mrs. Smith, both baby boomers in their late 60s, run a light manufacturing business in suburban Sydney. The business was "inherited" from Mrs. Smith's father in 2000, who started the business from scratch after World War II, originally operating from his garage.

About 18 years ago 30% of the business was sold to Rod Jones, the Sales Manager, a brilliant young employee, now also a director. Rod has added considerable value to the business over time.

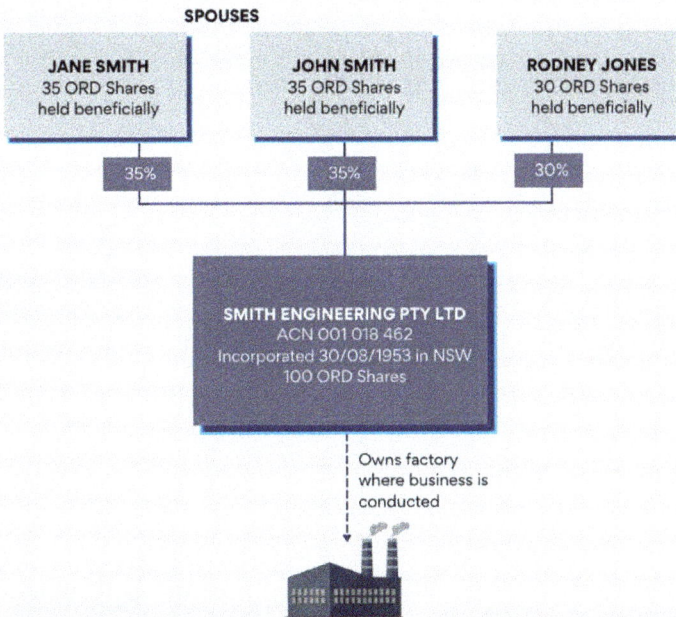

**SPOUSES**

| JANE SMITH | JOHN SMITH | RODNEY JONES |
| --- | --- | --- |
| 35 ORD Shares held beneficially | 35 ORD Shares held beneficially | 30 ORD Shares held beneficially |
| 35% | 35% | 30% |

**SMITH ENGINEERING PTY LTD**
ACN 001 018 462
Incorporated 30/08/1953 in NSW
100 ORD Shares

Owns factory where business is conducted

The company makes aluminum display stands for retail stores and has been stable and profitable for many years with several long- term and loyal customers. In August 2006, the Smiths purchased the factory from the landlord. The company owns several large machines used in the factory acquired over several years and the premises have been modified and customized to suit production.

## Business Succession

The Smiths' son, Gary, is the Production/Manufacturing Manager but they both know that he cannot run the business without help and expertise. Gary is very good practically but less so at managing finance. During 2015, he was appointed company General Manager and took over the day-to-day management of the business. Following this move, gross profit dropped nearly 10%; net profits were down by $300,000 and several key staff left because of his management style.

Both Mr. and Mrs. Smith are currently in good physical and mental health, but they are getting older and "slowing down."

## Financial Summary

The company has been slowly but consistently growing. Current turnover is a little over $8 million.  The company is quite profitable with the 2021 Financial Year producing a NOPAT (Net Operating Profit After Tax) of $1,214,796.

To finalize a Business Succession and Exit Plan, the owners approached their financial advisor and accountants who work in the same firm and who have been advising the family for many years. Whilst the family knows they need to do something, they really are unsure what options are available.

## Solution

The owners agree to start the process with a Business Insights Report giving them a comprehensive review and analysis of the various issues/value drivers before launching into a strategic succession plan based on the Capitaliz 21-step process.

# Step 1
# Goals and Outcomes

The first step is deciding what outcome you want for your retirement from the business. This will differ for everyone in terms of their financial and lifestyle goals, but there are some key factors to consider and discuss with your business advisors and financial planner. As we work through the steps in the book, you'll get a better understanding of what is realistically achievable from your business, however we'll start by identifying the main drivers and influencers in your exit plan.

## Initial Interview

Ask yourself the following questions. It might be useful to jot down your responses to discuss with your advisor.

1.  Do you have a valuation/sales price in mind for your business?

2.  Do you have personal/financial goals that your business sale needs to fund or make time for?

3.  When do you want to leave the business?

4.  Are you happy to stage your exit over several years?

5.  Do you want a lump sum to retire with, or could you work with several payments over time?

6.  Do you want to retain any ownership in the business?

7.  Do you want to transition the business to a family member?

8.  Do you have any key members of staff that would be keen to take on the business?

9.  Do you have a potential/interested buyer in mind?

10. Do you have a view of what the business will look like after you retire?

11. Are you interested in leaving a legacy?

12. What is your vision for the business in 10 years' time?

13. What do you plan to do post retirement?

Answering those questions honestly may make you feel quite ready and comfortable, or you may realize you have never really thought about these things before, let alone know how to make them happen. Some of these questions will prompt you to consider whether you have a strong preference for one form of action versus another. Going through the succession planning process will help you to aim for your preferred action, whilst also preparing you and making your business better able to adapt to alternative routes if needed.

Now that you have a clearer big picture view of where you'd like to be, let's investigate where you are.

# Case study

As an initial step, the owners are asked to provide information around long-term goals to ensure the business strategy meets their preferred/chosen outcomes and to ensure that their goals are compatible.

## Wheel of Life

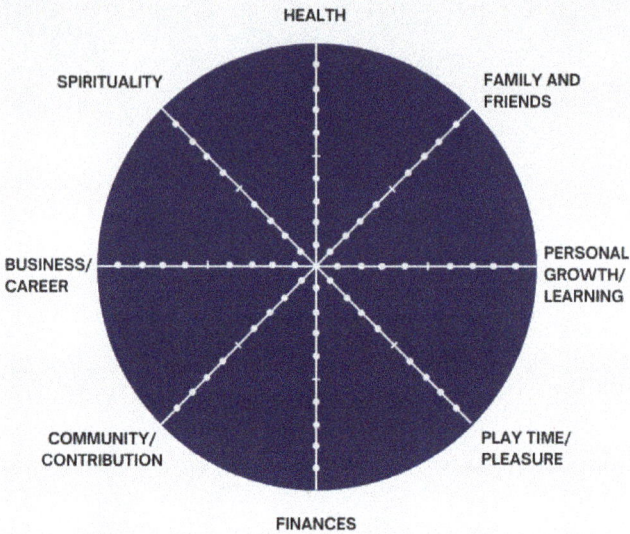

*The "Wheel of Life" is one way to discover what Jane, John, and Rodney value most in their lives and how satisfied they are with all areas of their life.*

## Goal Setting Workbook - Jane Smith

Jane has identified that she values her:

1. Faith
2. Family
3. Health

If she won the lottery, she would make large donations to several charities and then semi-retire.

Another question posed was "What would you do if you found out you only had 6 months to live?". Jane noted she would retire immediately, volunteer to help at her church, spend as much time as possible with her family and write a memoir. She would also have a living funeral.

Jane is then asked how satisfied she is in each area of the "Wheel of Life" and what she would need to do, to be completely satisfied.

These are summarized below:

- Financial - she is nearly completely satisfied
- Relationships with family and friends - Jane would like to spend more time with them, such as on a houseboat on the river.
- Health - she feels good for a woman in her 60's
- Spare time - she feels like she doesn't have any spare time
- Contributions to others - she would voluntarily work like she used to
- Spiritual development - starting to talk to God again
- Personal growth/learning - Jane might start reading one book a month
- Business/Career - Jane feels like she has achieved these goals

## Goal Setting Workbook - John Smith

The three things John values most in life are his grandchildren, his business, and his boat. He would buy a holiday home up the coast if he won the lottery. If he only had 6 months to live, he would fish every day and see as much of the grandchildren as he could.

John was also asked to identify his level of satisfaction for all areas on the "Wheel of Life" diagram.

He was concerned about his health, particularly his cholesterol and his family history of diabetes.

He is most concerned with his business/career. To feel completely satisfied he needs help with a proper handover to Rodney, so that Rodney can continue to operate the business without parents' involvement.

The things that give him the greatest feeling of self-worth was building up his business when his father-in-law passed it onto him.

**Goal Setting Workbook - Rodney Jones**

Rodney values his family, good times and memories and a Royal Enfield motorcycle the most in life. If he won the lottery, Rodney would retire as soon as he could transition out without hurting the business. He would also go on a trip around the world with his family. To feel completely satisfied with each section in the "Wheel of Life", he would need to achieve the following:

- Financial - have a lot more money in liquid assets
- Family/Friends - ensure his wife Pat is well
- Health - exercise more
- Play time/Pleasure - spend more time playing golf and rugby, feels he is working too much
- Business/Career - he is happy

# Step 2
## Fact Find

In Step 2, we'll start with looking at your business to determine the value and identify any issues, as well as strengths and opportunities and importantly, the value potential.

## Discovering what your business is all about

With your exit planning advisor, you'll go through the following questions:

- What does the business currently look like?
- What would it be worth in its current state?
- What are some of the risks in the business?
- What are the opportunities in the future?
- What profit is the business currently making?
- Are the financials up to date?
- What do you need to do to prepare for due diligence?

## A business versus a job

An important part of this process is establishing what do you have to sell. Do you have a business or are you self-employed?

In some cases, business owners who have started or bought a business have simply bought themselves a hobby that pays, or maybe a job. They may have bought a database or a few customer contracts (common in trades such as plumbing, mechanics), but the income is essentially derived from the business owner directly servicing clients. Robert Kiyosaki's definition of a job is 'Just Over Broke' because there's no equity value. The day you stop working, the money stops.

This type of business has little or no resale value unless you can find a way to replace yourself in the business with at least the same results. A good way to determine whether or not you have 'a business' is to consider how long you could be removed from it without affecting operations. If you could take significant chunks of time out and the business would continue to survive and produce income, you have a business. If you've got a position where you must be there all the time, you've got a job. The income stops when you stop.

It is important at this point to identify whether you have a 'job' so that you can spend time in your succession planning building a business or making the most of what you have. An advisor will help determine the best path for you.

# Case Study

The owners are asked to provide further business and background information by their advisor as part of the Capitaliz documentation requirement schedule.

### Benchmarking
The owners are asked to provide some basic benchmarking data about the industry, the business, and the employees. This includes being able to identify the roles each employee performs, how many staff perform that role, and how many hours per annum they carry out that role. This also needs to be done for all the owners of the businesses. This allows the software to benchmark performance using various KPIs against industry benchmarks.

### Addbacks
Further information is to be provided by the owners to "normalize" the earnings of the business. The following items are some examples of income and expenses to add back or adjust to the business earnings:

- Director's non-market salaries
- Unusual repair or maintenance cost
- Consultant fees not in the ordinary course of business
- One-off purchase/expenses
- Profit/loss on sale of a fixed asset
- Rent of facilities at above or below market value
- Donations/sponsorships
- Lawsuits and other legal fees
- Prepaid sales

The following tables list the information required for our fact find.

## 1. Company Information

### 💼 Company Information

**Company Information**

| | |
|---|---|
| General Information | TO BE STARTED |
| Organisational Chart (optional) | TO BE STARTED |
| Strategy documents (optional) | TO BE STARTED |
| Company Structure Diagram (optional) | COMPLETE |

## 2. Financial Information

### ⓢ Financial Information

**Financial Information**

| | |
|---|---|
| Benchmarking Questionnaire | TO BE STARTED |
| Financial Statements, Tax Returns and Payroll Reports | COMPLETE |
| Budgets/Projections (optional) | TO BE STARTED |
| Adjustments and Normalization | COMPLETE |

## 3. Non-financial Information

### 📄 Non-Financial Information

**Non-Financial Information**

| | |
|---|---|
| Beta-Factor Risk Assessment | COMPLETE |
| Foundation | COMPLETE |
| Strategic Growth | COMPLETE |

## 4. Stakeholder Information

### 👥 Stakeholder Information

**Stakeholder Information**

| | |
|---|---|
| Goal Setting Questionnaire | TO BE STARTED |
| Fact Find Questionnaire | TO BE STARTED |

## 5. Additional Notes & Clarifications

✎ **Additional Notes & Clarifications**

**Additional Notes & Clarifications**

Client Notes (private)                      TO BE STARTED

Clarifications from Analyst                  TO BE STARTED

Effective Tax Rate                           TO BE STARTED

Business
Insights
Report

Step 3 is the point at which a comprehensive analysis and diagnosis is performed on your business. We do a deep dive into the detail of your business, assessing it for risks and identifying gaps that may prevent you from maximizing your return. Then we'll identify the key areas that need action and show you how to maximize your business value by following our process.

## Structural Review

First, we look at how your business has been set up and structured, for example, who or what entity owns the business.

But over time, as the business grows, you purchase other assets such as equipment or real estate. Some businesses buy the premises they operate from, and the real estate may be held in the trading entity, along with a stake in another business or a significant piece of equipment, with no separation of risk and assets.

Part of our job is to minimize the risks with the right ownership structure. To many people, asset protection means being able to control assets or have access to assets which they do not actually own, so that if they are sued, the assets are not at risk. Common examples are assets being owned by a family company or trust or being placed in the spouse's name.

The key is separation. Wherever possible, quarantine the assets from the risk, especially capital appreciating assets like property, by creating separate structures. Where husband and wife are both directors, they are both at risk individually. So, we need to find a way to protect them too. It's not that the wrong structure has been set up, rather that the business has changed over the years, increased in value, and taken on assets and risks, and the original structure is no longer appropriate. Another aspect of asset protection is having adequate insurance cover, and good systems in place to prevent and minimize risk.

We also look at where we want those assets to end up. Perhaps you want to keep the business premises and rent them out to the new owners to create an ongoing income stream. If so, you won't want it sitting in a trading entity, but more likely in a self-managed superannuation fund, trust, or other structure.

Here we'll work closely with your financial planner to ensure you get the most benefit from your assets.

## Financial Analysis

As an accountant I tend to focus on the financial analysis next, but I'd also argue that it's not the most important area in determining value. We do, however, need to get a good understanding of how the business is performing. We use a financial analysis tool to provide the business owners a snapshot of the financial performance and the areas for improvement.

The following diagram shows a typical overview of the financial position of a small business. It assesses the business's profitability, cashflow, debt levels, efficiency, and highlights the performance of each of the measures using a traffic light system of green for good, amber for caution and red for watch out!

The tool focuses on measurements that are relevant to your business - in this example nineteen out of twenty-two measures were favorable, so the business owner can see clearly that they need to focus their attention on improving the three unfavorable measures – Inventory (WIP) Days, Activity Ratio, and Asset Turnover Ratio. This business scored an A-, which is quite good for a small to medium business.

It is important to know the key financial drivers and performance indicators at any stage of your business so that you can step in and make improvements. This is of course crucial when you are preparing your business for sale. The potential buyer will look not only at the financial performance of your business, but also how well you manage the financial data, and how quickly you act on key financial indicators to improve performance.

FY 2021

# Financial Scorecard

**A-**

| Liquidity | 2 out of 2 |
|---|---|
| ✓ Current Ratio | |
| ✓ Quick Ratio | |

| Working Capital | 2 out of 3 |
|---|---|
| ✓ Account Receivable Days | |
| ✓ Account Payable Days | |
| ✗ Inventory (WIP) Days | |

| Profitability Ratios | 3 out of 3 |
|---|---|
| ✓ Gross Profit Margin | |
| ✓ Profitability % | |
| ✓ NOPAT % | |

| Efficiency Ratios | 4 out of 4 |
|---|---|
| ✓ Return On Equity | |
| ✓ Return On Total Assets | |
| ✓ Return On Capital Employed | |
| ✓ ECROCE | |

| Asset Usage | 2 out of 4 |
|---|---|
| ✗ Activity Ratio | |
| ✗ Asset Turnover Ratio | |
| ✓ GM Return on Inventory | |
| ✓ Working Capital Absorption Rate | |

| Gearing | 2 out of 2 |
|---|---|
| ✓ Interest Coverage Ratio | |
| ✓ Debt to Equity Ratio | |

| Other | 4 out of 4 |
|---|---|
| ✓ Sustainable Growth Rate | |
| ✓ Marginal Cash | |
| ✓ Earnings per Share | |
| ✓ Free Cash Flow | |

Capitaliz

## Benchmarking and Profit Gap

Benchmarking is a process of comparing your business metrics with those of other similar businesses. Not many business owners think of benchmarking their business, and most do not have access to data to be able to do this. At Succession Plus, we identify the key performance indicators in your business and benchmark them against industry averages to identify areas of improvement, or 'the profit gap' between where you are and where you could be.

Benchmarking uses largely financial data but also uses statistics such as the number of employees, floor space utilized, total equipment, or assets. Some of these measures of efficiency aren't immediately apparent from your management accounts, but a buyer will want to understand how you are positioned in the market to assess your relative value.

If, for example, you operate an accounting firm, where your profit depends on billing time for services, benchmarking would look at billable hours, total fees earned per full time employee (or equivalent) and overheads. The graphs below show benchmark reporting for a professional services firm versus industry averages.

## Average debtor days

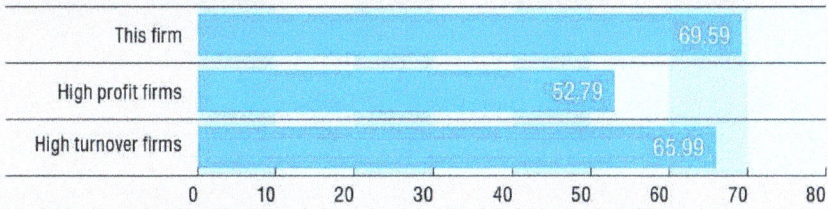

| | | |
|---|---|---|
| This firm | | 69.59 |
| High profit firms | | 52.79 |
| High turnover firms | | 65.99 |

| 0 | 10 | 20 | 30 | 40 | 50 | 60 | 70 | 80 |

This firm's debt collection is slower than the industry average, which may lead to cashflow issues.

## Average NPAT per principal

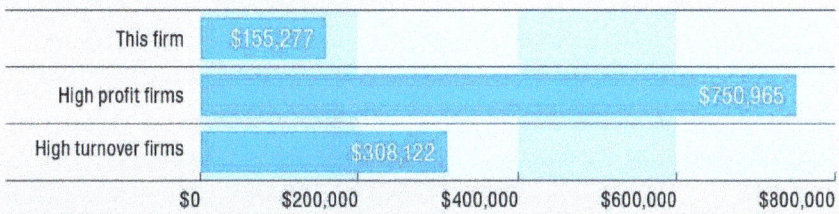

| | | |
|---|---|---|
| This firm | $155,277 | |
| High profit firms | | $750,965 |
| High turnover firms | $308,122 | |

| $0 | $200,000 | $400,000 | $600,000 | $800,000 |

This firm's average net profit after tax (NPAT) per principal is much lower than the industry average. While this may be largely driven by the size and profile of the firm, it prompts additional analysis into pricing, volume of work, and utilization of staff and costs.

## Minor overheads as % total income

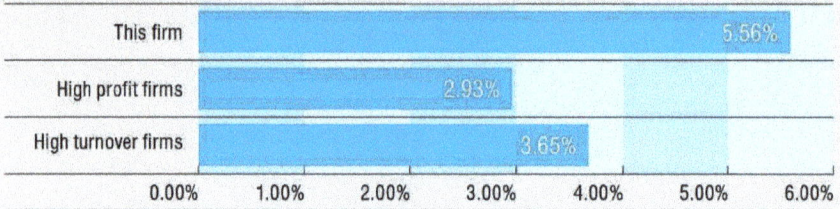

| | |
|---|---|
| This firm | 5.56% |
| High profit firms | 2.93% |
| High turnover firms | 3.65% |

0.00%  1.00%  2.00%  3.00%  4.00%  5.00%  6.00%

This firm spends more of its total income on minor overheads than the industry average, which will put pressure on profit.

While the firm may be too small to reach the industry averages, benchmarking gives us a good starting point to highlight where we need to look deeper to improve the future performance of the business.

When we benchmarked one of our Sydney clients, a professional services firm, we found the IT costs were significantly higher than its industry competitors. Digging deeper, we saw that the firm's computers were 15 years old, and all the systems were old and slow, which meant the maintenance contractor was coming in almost every day to fix something. On the other hand, depreciation was much lower than competitors as the assets were all fully written down long ago.

A buyer considering this business will need to factor in significant capital outlay to replace the IT assets, however, can also expect to spend less in maintenance costs as a result, therefore increasing profit.

When we benchmark a business we calculate the potential profit gap, which is the profit you could achieve if you were operating at industry average levels. Simplistically, if you produce a product at $1 and sell it at $2 you are making $1, or a 50% margin. If your competitor is selling the same thing for $2 but it costs $0.75 to produce, he is making $1.25 or 62.5% margin. The profit gap is 12.5% or 25 cents. Benchmarking assumes that you should be able to operate at roughly the same level as industry averages.

Sometimes there is a significant gap between the current profitability and profitability that could be achieved at maximum efficiency. Once we work out where the business is over or underperforming or overspending, we focus on resolving individual issues to close the gap, improving profitability and value.

## Example Profit Gap Table

| Your Profit Gaps relative to the Most Profitable firms: | This Business | High Profit Firms Average | Profit Gap Relative to High Proft Firms |
|---|---|---|---|
| If you could achieve the average level of fees per person | | $245,000 | |
| then your firm's present fees of | $3,800,000 | | |
| would need a total personnel of | 15.51 | | |
| but you presently have total personnel of | 19 | | |
| so you are overstaffed by | | | 3.49 |
| and at your average salary cost per employee of | $65,000 | | |
| your salary-related Profit Gap is: | | | $226,837 |
| If you could achieve the average level of non-salary overheads | 25.80% | 24.00% | |
| you should reduce your overheads by | | | 1.8% |
| then on your present turnover of | $3,800,000 | | |
| you are over spending by | | | $68,400 |
| You asset turnover is presently | 1.90 | 2 | |
| but your current revenue of | $3,800,000 | | |
| suggests you should have assets of | | | $1,900,000 |
| Currently you have assets (net of any loans to owners) of | $2,100,000 | | |
| So you could look to reduce total assets by | | | $200,000 |
| If this could save you interest at, say, | 9.00% | | |
| Then you'd close a Profit Gap of: | | | $18,000 |

| Your total Profit Gap: | Relative to high profit firms |
|---|---|
| 1. Bringing your personnel numbers back could yield | $226,837 |
| 2. Reducing non-salary overheads could yield | $68,400 |
| 3. Reducing your investment in the firm could yield | $18,000 |
| So your total Profit Gap is | $313,237 |
| Which is ... of your current profit level | 43% |

## Non-financial Analysis

Our non-financial evaluation is an interview process with owners and key staff to take a good look at the operations of the business and determine where there is risk. It will be these areas that ultimately affect the multiple you can achieve on sale. In our experience, these are also the areas that are largely in your control, and some can be improved relatively easily.

Some of the interview questions are as follows:

1. Do you have an up-to-date company profile and website?

2. Do you have all your intellectual property registered and up to date? For example, business name registrations, trademarks, patents.

3. Are your financial statements, BAS, payroll, and tax returns in order?

4. Do you have monthly or quarterly management accounts?

5. Do you have an annual budget for the current year?

6. Do you have monthly management meetings, and do you have minutes of those meetings?

7. Do you have robust accounting systems that allow you to run reports on top customers, top suppliers, debtors, creditors, KPIs?

8. Do you have employee agreements in place for all your employees?

9. Are you meeting your obligations re employees - leave balances, superannuation contribution, award rates, payroll tax, workers compensation?

10. Are all your vehicles registered, insured and lease payments up to date?

11. Do you have the lease agreements for your premises?

12. Are your company registration documents up to date? E.g., articles of association, shareholder agreements etc.

13. Have you documented key processes, job descriptions and procedures (such as a safety manual, induction manual) in your business?

14. Do you have a board of directors or advisory board, and do you communicate regularly?

15. Has your IT system been reviewed lately to ensure it meets your needs?

16. Do you have back-up facilities in place and a disaster recovery plan?

A prospective buyer will see the non-financial measures of your business as a reflection of how you manage your business. Your attention to detail and compliance, your ability to plan and execute, how easily the business can operate without you, the quality of your staff, and whether they are locked into the business or not. They will also look not just at your financial performance, but how well you manage and use financial information.

The diagram below shows an architecture business with an E rating on Strategic Growth. In the top middle we have risk management, and this business has a red tick for key person risk. This is usual in small to medium businesses, which are usually very dependent on founders and key people. In this business, there are four architects, which means the business could not continue to operate if one left.

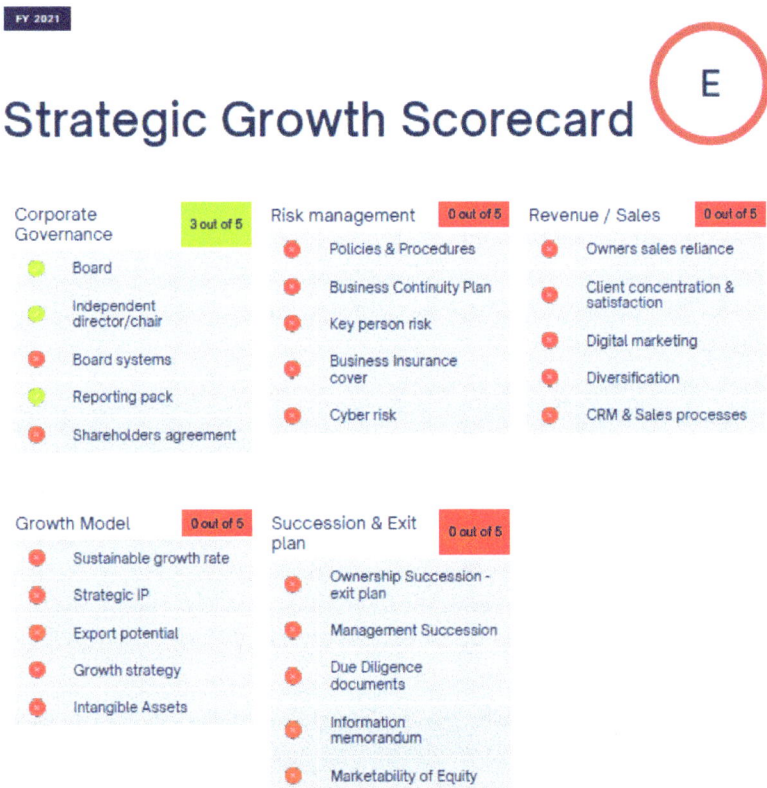

FY 2021

# Strategic Growth Scorecard  (E)

**Corporate Governance** — 3 out of 5
- Board
- Independent director/chair
- Board systems
- Reporting pack
- Shareholders agreement

**Risk management** — 0 out of 5
- Policies & Procedures
- Business Continuity Plan
- Key person risk
- Business Insurance cover
- Cyber risk

**Revenue / Sales** — 0 out of 5
- Owners sales reliance
- Client concentration & satisfaction
- Digital marketing
- Diversification
- CRM & Sales processes

**Growth Model** — 0 out of 5
- Sustainable growth rate
- Strategic IP
- Export potential
- Growth strategy
- Intangible Assets

**Succession & Exit plan** — 0 out of 5
- Ownership Succession - exit plan
- Management Succession
- Due Diligence documents
- Information memorandum
- Marketability of Equity

This company doesn't have a board structure in place, which would be a disadvantage down the track due to the apparent governance risk. They have no shareholders or buy/sell agreement, which could cause quite significant issues if one partner leaves the business, gets sick or is hit by the proverbial bus. Like many small companies, this business does not have a business or succession plan.

FY 2021

# Foundation Scorecard

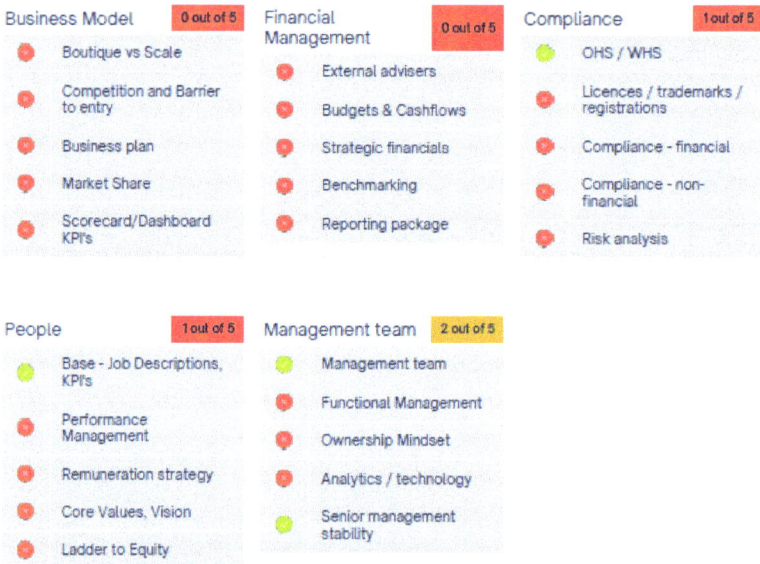

E+

| Business Model | 0 out of 5 |
| --- | --- |
| Boutique vs Scale | |
| Competition and Barrier to entry | |
| Business plan | |
| Market Share | |
| Scorecard/Dashboard KPI's | |

| Financial Management | 0 out of 5 |
| --- | --- |
| External advisers | |
| Budgets & Cashflows | |
| Strategic financials | |
| Benchmarking | |
| Reporting package | |

| Compliance | 1 out of 5 |
| --- | --- |
| OHS / WHS | |
| Licences / trademarks / registrations | |
| Compliance - financial | |
| Compliance - non-financial | |
| Risk analysis | |

| People | 1 out of 5 |
| --- | --- |
| Base - Job Descriptions, KPI's | |
| Performance Management | |
| Remuneration strategy | |
| Core Values, Vision | |
| Ladder to Equity | |

| Management team | 2 out of 5 |
| --- | --- |
| Management team | |
| Functional Management | |
| Ownership Mindset | |
| Analytics / technology | |
| Senior management stability | |

You can see in the diagram above that the company is also performing poorly in almost all foundational areas – business model, financial management, people, compliance, and management team. They haven't had the business benchmarked so they don't really have a clear direction to determine the future value of the business. They also don't have a clear remuneration strategy or an employee share plan, which does expose some risk of staff turnover despite some good HR practices.

These diagrams clearly show the risks in the business and helps us to prioritize action. For example, we would certainly recommend having a shareholders' agreement and buy/sell agreement prepared.

# Valuation

Once we've completed the analysis we arrive at a business valuation figure, and we'll hit the pause button to protect the wealth that's already been created before we think about growing that value to reach your retirement goals.

A major part of that protection involves decreasing business risk. First, let's look at the mechanics behind valuations and some of the jargon associated with it.

### Financial Valuations

There are several ways to value a business in a largely mathematical way, arriving at a financial valuation. No matter which method is used (except for liquidation), and who prepares the valuation (be it an accountant, potential buyer, advisor, or valuation expert), the various outcomes of a financial valuation will be largely consistent. The financial value should reflect the market value of the business, and what it would be worth to someone who takes it on and continues to run it in much the same way, capitalizing on the potential identified.

A strategic valuation on the other hand, does not necessarily represent the market value of the business, but what that business is worth to the acquirer for strategic reasons. A strategic buyer is likely to pay well above the financial valuation of the business.

The following are examples of financial valuations.

### EBIT Multiple

An EBIT multiple valuations is derived by multiplying the annual ongoing profit of a business by a multiple. For example, a business that generates $500,000 per year and is valued at a multiple of 2 should achieve a sales price of $1 million. Despite being a mathematical calculation, many non-financial drivers impact the multiple, while the main financial driver is the profit figure.

The main drivers affecting the multiple are risk and potential. A business with low risk and high potential can achieve a high multiple, while a business with high risk and limited potential will achieve a low multiple.

Small businesses in Australia generally sell for multiples of around 2-3, but in recent times many businesses have been sold for multiples of less than 1; that is the business owner takes less than a year's profit to have the business taken off their hands.

The data below from Merge Market tracks transactions in the United States, and it tracks transactions based on different sized businesses but also over a period. There are two key things you can learn very quickly from the table. The first thing is larger businesses sell for more. Why is that? It's because risk is lower, and the predictability of future maintainable earnings is much easier to do in a large business than it is in a very small business.

The top line is businesses worth less than $20 million. Now we're talking about a small business that might be worth $2 million then the multiple's obviously much lower. In fact, multiples currently two and a half to four times is quite common for small businesses. So, you can see here the larger the business, the higher the multiple.

You can also see over the last few years, going back as far as 2011 and 2012, which is only a couple of years after the end of the GFC, typical multiples were around seven, but as we come forward to recent data, we're looking at multiples up around nine and ten.

*Source: SSP Capital IQ, Mergemarket, Grant Thornton*

| Revenue range | No. of deals | Current Dealtracker median | Prior 2018 Dealtracker median | Prior 2017 Dealtracker median | Prior 2016 Dealtracker median | Prior 2014 Dealtracker median | Prior 2012 Dealtracker median | Prior 2011 Dealtracker median | Historical Dealtracker average |
|---|---|---|---|---|---|---|---|---|---|
| Less than $20 million | 27 | 6.3x | 5.1x | 7.2x | 5.5x | 5.5x | 4.9x | 6.1x | 5.8x |
| Between $20 million to $50 million | 16 | 6.2x | 6.6x | 5.9x | 8.8x | 6.7x | 6.1x | 6.5x | 6.7x |
| Between $50 million to $100 million | 11 | 11.5x | 8.2x | 8.9x | 6.1x | 8.0x | 7.0x | 7.9x | 8.2x |
| Between $100 million to $200 million | 19 | 8.9x | 12.6x | 7.6x | 10.8x | 7.8x | 8.7x | 7.5x | 9.1x |
| Between $200 million to $500 million | 8 | 8.2x | 13.2x | 10.2x | 8.5x | 8.8x | 7.0x | 8.7x | 9.2x |
| Over $500 million | 14 | 10.8x | 11.4x | 11.9x | 10.9x | 7.1x | 8.9x | 9.8x | 10.1x |
| Median (overall) | | 8.1x | 7.1x | 9.0x | 7.8x | 7.3x | 7.5x | 7.5x | 7.8x |
| Total | 95 | | | | | | | | |

*Note: Multiple in this data refers to a multiple of EBITDA.*

# Valuation Theory and Methodology

How do we value businesses? What is it that we use? What's the theory that sits behind that? There are a few critical areas to look at.

It's a little bit like the real estate story around. You can get as many valuations and appraisals for your property as you want, but at the end of the day, it's only worth what someone's willing to pay. But of course, there's always a difference between book value or a written down value or a theoretical value that comes out of a report and what your business is worth.

Sometimes people will pay much more and occasionally they'll pay or want to pay much less. We understand how those things relate and how that relates to the value of your business. So, let's start with some basic concepts.

## Risk and Reward

Risk and reward - the two parts of the equation that we need to factor in. But within these there are many factors to consider, as not all risk and not all returns are created equal.

Business valuation is often described as "more art than science" but it does not need to be. Completing a business valuation is essentially answering two key questions – what return can I get from my investment and how risky is it?

In a listed company, this is done regularly and updated daily, or more often, and is relatively easy to do. It is also easy in most listed companies to "draw comparisons" (the property equivalent of viewing recent sales in your street/area). In smaller privately held business neither aspect is easy.

### What is my return?

This should be about finding out what is the "normal" profit/earnings you can expect to get, adding back unusual items or a non-market rent paid to a related entity. Once we go through this process, we can work out the "normalized earnings" – the return.

### What is my risk?

This is about working out the various risks that affect that return. Again, in SMEs, there are far more risks than listed companies – no structured reporting, often no audited accounts and more importantly, often the business is largely or entirely dependent upon the owner or family, sometimes the business is highly susceptible to new technology or disruption, and often the business has key employees who are not "locked in". All these factors make your return riskier.

Higher risk = lower valuation multiples and therefore lower business value.

So, the main pitfall is to focus only on one side of the valuation equation - the return - and in fact the variable that has the most effect is the other side - the risk!

### EBITDA or NOPAT

A lot of clients ask about valuation methods and the underlying metric we use to value their business: EBITDA (Earnings Before Interest, Tax, Depreciation and Amortization), which is commonly used and often referred to especially around listed companies, or NOPAT (Net Operating Profit after Tax). We prefer NOPAT and we use it in all our reports and valuations.

There's a lot of debate around why you would use that compared to EBIT or compared to EBITDA. And the reason that we use NOPAT is because that includes everything. Any of those other measures like EBIT and EBITDA, by definition, is earnings before something - earnings before interest, earnings before tax, earnings before depreciation, and earnings before amortization. If you think about it from a very practical measurement, forget the theory for a second, there is no business you can run today and completely ignore interest, tax, depreciation, and amortization. They are all a cost. Some of them are accounting treatments of costs, but they're all a real physical cost to a business. So, to run a valuation based on numbers that exclude a whole list of actual costs, is a bit of a fantasy.

To calculate the true underlying value of the business, surely, we need to do so with everything factored into the calculation.

## Reverse Due Diligence

An important step in the preparation process is reverse due diligence, a process that is very similar to the due diligence a buyer or an investor would undertake when looking at your business, so it will help you enormously in getting prepared. We give you a comprehensive list of all the things that we need to compile in terms of documentation. We can then identify any areas where we've got gaps, where we've got information that's out of date or where we can't find original documentation.

It's surprising how many business owners come to us asking us to sell their business quickly, yet when we give them a list of the information we need – on average it will take them six to eight weeks to collect it all! The information we request are the management accounts - balance sheets, profit and loss statements, and a breakdown of clients, leases, contracts, and agreements. Business owners often don't have it, can't get it, or must wait for their accountant to prepare it. Once we do receive the documentation we are after, it can sometimes prove impossible to reconcile with the BAS statements which have already been submitted.

- It is important to be on top of this early on - it will make your business look much more professional and much less risky if you are on the front foot when you are asked to provide information.

Focus on getting the following up to date and ready for inspection:

- Financial statements and management accounts
- Trend analysis for the last 12 months
- Top 10 customers - spend, margins, terms
- Legal documentation - shareholders certificates up to date, all licenses and IP current
- Employee contracts up to date and entitlements properly accounted for.
- Google analytics
- Social media analysis

# Case Study

In reviewing the financials, a few key points were highlighted by the accountant's analysis:

1.  The business is performing well financially but performance could be improved.

2.  The downturn in 2020 would raise concern with potential buyers/investors and needs to be explained.

3.  The financial statements are recast to allow further and more detailed analysis.

4.  The accountants referred the client directly to a Capitaliz accredited advisor for specialized advice to design and implement a business succession and exit plan.

# Financial Analysis

## Original Financials

FY 2021

# Original Financials

| Profit & Loss | 2018 | 2019 | 2020 | 2021 |
|---|---|---|---|---|
| Income | $5,771,884 | $6,561,310 | $7,481,200 | $8,093,000 |
| Cost of Sales | $3,173,500 | $3,377,800 | $4,501,740 | $4,101,720 |
| Gross Profit | $2,598,384 | $3,183,510 | $2,979,460 | $3,991,280 |
| Total Operating Expenses | $1,888,038 | $2,019,032 | $2,230,881 | $2,622,516 |
| Net Operating Profit | $710,346 | $1,164,478 | $748,579 | $1,368,764 |
| Other Income | $0 | $0 | $0 | $0 |
| Net Profit Before Tax | $710,346 | $1,164,478 | $748,579 | $1,368,764 |
| Tax Expenses | $195,345 | $320,231 | $205,859 | $355,878 |
| Net Profit After Tax | $515,001 | $844,247 | $542,720 | $1,012,886 |
| Dividend paids or declared/Profit Distribution | $0 | $579,173 | $328,000 | $674,501 |
| Retained Earnings | $515,001 | $265,074 | $214,720 | $338,385 |
| Balance Sheet | | | | |
| Cash And Cash Equivalents | $213,451 | $254,758 | $230,456 | $214,657 |
| Other Current Assets | $1,265,254 | $1,433,254 | $1,462,639 | $1,591,284 |
| Other Non-Current Assets | $117,664 | $24,065 | $208,446 | $222,408 |
| Fixed Assets | $2,294,612 | $2,386,495 | $2,447,714 | $2,545,600 |
| Total Assets | $3,890,981 | $4,098,572 | $4,349,255 | $4,573,949 |
| Current Liabilities | $578,035 | $608,034 | $743,500 | $733,636 |
| Non-Current Liabilities | $1,917,946 | $1,830,464 | $1,730,961 | $1,627,134 |
| Total Liabilities | $2,495,981 | $2,438,498 | $2,474,461 | $2,360,770 |
| Net Assets | $1,395,000 | $1,660,074 | $1,874,794 | $2,213,179 |
| Accumulated Retained Earnings | $1,394,000 | $1,659,074 | $1,873,794 | $2,212,179 |
| Share Capital | $1,000 | $1,000 | $1,000 | $1,000 |
| Total Equity | $1,395,000 | $1,660,074 | $1,874,794 | $2,213,179 |

Capitaliz

**Addbacks Schedule**

# Addbacks

| Addbacks | 2018 | 2019 | 2020 | 2021 |
|---|---|---|---|---|
| (A) Original net profit before tax | $710,346 | $1,164,478 | $748,579 | $1,368,764 |
| (B) Add backs to profit | | | | |
| Personal expenses paid for by company (non-business related) | $24,000 | $30,000 | $25,000 | $45,000 |
| Donations | $5,000 | $8,000 | $0 | $10,000 |
| Entertainment | $15,000 | $22,000 | $15,000 | $24,000 |
| (C) Deductions from profit | | | | |
| Total Market Remuneration for all Owners | $120,000 | $122,000 | $125,000 | $130,000 |
| Market Rent Adjustment | $60,028 | $62,238 | $77,804 | $113,302 |
| (D) Net add backs and deductions (B-C) | -$136,028 | -$124,238 | -$162,804 | -$164,302 |
| (E) Normalised net profit before tax (A+D) | $574,318 | $1,040,240 | $585,775 | $1,204,462 |
| (F1) Notionally imputed tax (E x effective tax rate) | $0 | $0 | $0 | $0 |
| (F2) Original tax expenses | $195,345 | $320,231 | $205,859 | $355,878 |
| (F) Net tax adjustment | -$195,345 | -$320,231 | -$205,859 | -$355,878 |
| (G) Total Adjustments to accounts (D-F) | $59,317 | $195,993 | $43,055 | $191,576 |
| (H) Normalized net profit after tax (E-F1) | $574,318 | $1,040,240 | $585,775 | $1,204,462 |
| (I) Net interest | $7,370 | $7,751 | $8,872 | $10,334 |
| (J) Normalized EBIT (E+I) | $581,688 | $1,047,991 | $594,647 | $1,214,796 |

Capitaliz

## Addbacks and Adjustments

In most small businesses, there are items in the accounts which are not typical of "normal" business trading, and which need to be adjusted to provide a more accurate picture of the business and its financial performance. To do this, we create a table of adjustments and addbacks.

Typically, these relate to owners' salary/wages (which are rarely at market value), superannuation for owners and family members, non-market expenses for related parties and other "one-off" or non-recurring expenses, for example, a large legal case.

## Normalized Profit and Loss Statement

`FY 2021`

# Normalised Profit & Loss

| | 2018 | 2019 | 2020 | 2021 |
|---|---|---|---|---|
| **Revenue** | | | | |
| Sales | $5,771,884 | $6,561,310 | $7,481,200 | $8,093,000 |
| **Cost Of Sales** | | | | |
| COS Goods | - | - | - | - |
| COS Other | $3,173,500 | $3,377,800 | $4,501,740 | $4,101,720 |
| COS Fixed | - | - | - | - |
| Non-Cash COS | - | - | - | - |
| **Gross Profit** | $2,598,384 | $3,183,510 | $2,979,460 | $3,991,280 |
| **Expenses** | | | | |
| Fixed | $2,000,668 | $2,133,281 | $2,347,009 | $2,742,182 |
| Variable | $16,028 | $2,238 | $37,804 | $34,302 |
| Non-Cash Expenses | - | - | - | - |
| **Total Expenses** | $2,016,696 | $2,135,519 | $2,384,813 | $2,776,484 |
| **Operating Income** | $581,688 | $1,047,991 | $594,647 | $1,214,796 |
| Other Income | - | - | - | - |
| **Earnings Before Interest & Tax** | $581,688 | $1,047,991 | $594,647 | $1,214,796 |
| **Interest** | | | | |
| Interest Expense | $7,370 | $7,751 | $8,872 | $10,334 |
| Other Loan Interest | - | - | - | - |
| Interest Received (Excess Cash) | - | - | - | - |
| **Net Interest** | $7,370 | $7,751 | $8,872 | $10,334 |
| Tax Expense (Notional) | - | - | - | - |
| **Net Profit After Tax** | $574,318 | $1,040,240 | $585,775 | $1,204,462 |
| Adjustments | $59,317 | $195,993 | $43,055 | $191,576 |
| Net Income | $515,001 | $844,247 | $542,720 | $1,012,886 |
| Dividends Paid | - | $579,173 | $328,000 | $674,501 |
| **Retained Income** | $515,001 | $265,074 | $214,720 | $338,385 |
| Adjustments To Retained Income | - | - | - | - |

Capitaliz

**Normalized Finance Balance Sheet**

`FY 2021`

# Finance Balance Sheet

| Equity | 2018 | 2019 | 2020 | 2021 |
|---|---|---|---|---|
| Share Capital | $1,000 | $1,000 | $1,000 | $1,000 |
| Accum. Retained Income | $1,394,000 | $1,659,074 | $1,873,794 | $2,212,179 |
| Reserves | - | - | - | - |
| Other Equity | - | - | - | - |
| **Total Equity** | **$1,395,000** | **$1,660,074** | **$1,874,794** | **$2,213,179** |
| **Non-Current Liabilities (Ex Debt)** | | | | |
| Deferred Tax | - | - | - | - |
| Dividends (Other Funding) | - | - | - | - |
| Other Non-Current Liabilities | - | - | - | - |
| Total Non-Current Liabilities (Ex Debt) | - | - | - | - |
| **Debt** | | | | |
| Short Term Debt | $105,000 | $83,674 | $108,000 | $107,000 |
| Long Term Debt | $1,917,946 | $1,830,464 | $1,730,961 | $1,627,134 |
| Other Loans | - | - | - | - |
| Excess Cash | - | - | - | - |
| **Total Debt** | **$2,022,946** | **$1,914,138** | **$1,838,961** | **$1,734,134** |
| **Total Finance** | **$3,417,946** | **$3,574,212** | **$3,713,755** | **$3,947,313** |

Capitaliz

**Normalized Operations Balance Sheet**

FY 2021

# Operations Balance Sheet

| Current Assets | 2018 | 2019 | 2020 | 2021 |
|---|---|---|---|---|
| Cash And Cash Equivalents | $213,451 | $254,758 | $230,456 | $214,657 |
| Accounts Receivable | $474,401 | $539,286 | $922,340 | $665,178 |
| Inventory | $264,458 | $281,483 | $346,651 | $341,810 |
| Other Current Assets | $526,395 | $612,485 | $193,648 | $584,296 |
| **Total Current Assets** | **$1,478,705** | **$1,688,012** | **$1,693,095** | **$1,805,941** |
| **Current Liabilities** | | | | |
| Accounts Payable | $391,253 | $416,441 | $555,009 | $505,692 |
| Tax Liability | $23,818 | $29,183 | $27,311 | $36,587 |
| Other Current Liabilities | $57,964 | $78,736 | $53,180 | $84,357 |
| **Total Current Liabilities** | **$473,035** | **$524,360** | **$635,500** | **$626,636** |
| **Working Capital** | **$1,005,670** | **$1,163,652** | **$1,057,595** | **$1,179,305** |
| **Non-Current Assets** | | | | |
| Fixed Assets | $2,294,612 | $2,386,495 | $2,447,714 | $2,545,600 |
| Intangibles | - | - | - | - |
| Other Non-Current Assets | $117,664 | $24,065 | $208,446 | $222,408 |
| Investments | - | - | - | - |
| **Total Non-Current Assets** | **$2,412,276** | **$2,410,560** | **$2,656,160** | **$2,768,008** |
| **Total Operations** | **$3,417,946** | **$3,574,212** | **$3,713,755** | **$3,947,313** |

Capitaliz

A full review of adjusted financial statements allows the financial information to be scored and areas of underperformance highlighted. A score of A- is generally quite good for an SME.

**Financial Scorecard**

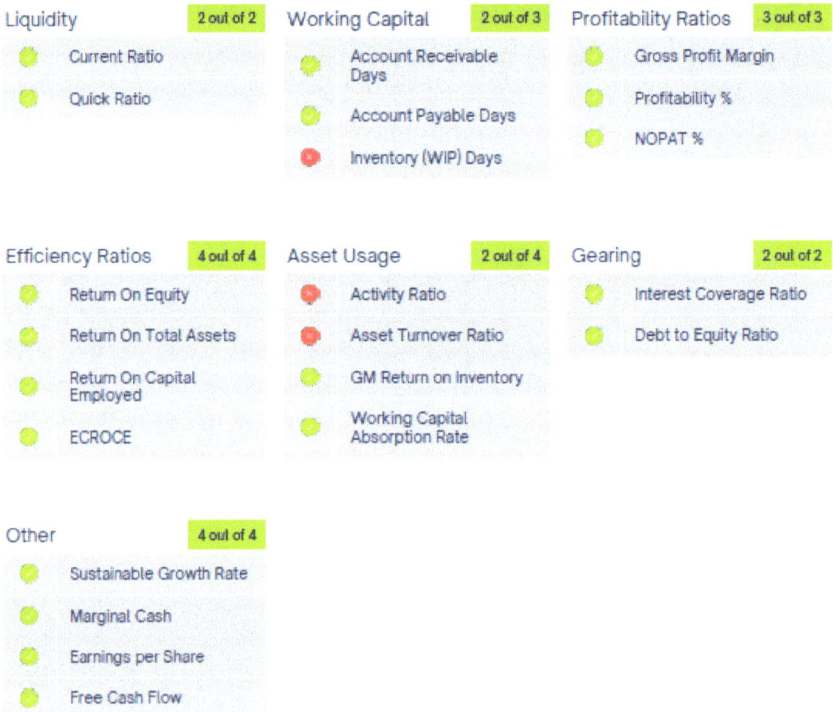

# Financial Scorecard

A-

| Liquidity | 2 out of 2 |
|---|---|
| Current Ratio | |
| Quick Ratio | |

| Working Capital | 2 out of 3 |
|---|---|
| Account Receivable Days | |
| Account Payable Days | |
| Inventory (WIP) Days | |

| Profitability Ratios | 3 out of 3 |
|---|---|
| Gross Profit Margin | |
| Profitability % | |
| NOPAT % | |

| Efficiency Ratios | 4 out of 4 |
|---|---|
| Return On Equity | |
| Return On Total Assets | |
| Return On Capital Employed | |
| ECROCE | |

| Asset Usage | 2 out of 4 |
|---|---|
| Activity Ratio | |
| Asset Turnover Ratio | |
| GM Return on Inventory | |
| Working Capital Absorption Rate | |

| Gearing | 2 out of 2 |
|---|---|
| Interest Coverage Ratio | |
| Debt to Equity Ratio | |

| Other | 4 out of 4 |
|---|---|
| Sustainable Growth Rate | |
| Marginal Cash | |
| Earnings per Share | |
| Free Cash Flow | |

**Financial Ratios**

FY 2021

# Financial Ratios

| Liquidity | Value | Target | Result |
|---|---|---|---|
| Current Ratio | 2.88:1 | 2.00:1 | 🟢 |
| Quick Ratio | 1.40:1 | 1.00:1 | 🟢 |

| Working Capital | Value | Target | Result |
|---|---|---|---|
| Account Receivable Days | 30.0 days | 45.0 days | 🟢 |
| Account Payable Days | 45.0 days | 55.0 days | 🟢 |
| Inventory (WIP) Days | 30.4 days | 25.0 days | 🔴 |

| Profitability Ratios | Value | Target | Result |
|---|---|---|---|
| Gross Profit Margin | 49.32% | 45.00% | 🟢 |
| Profitability % | 15.01% | 15.00% | 🟢 |
| NOPAT % | 15.04% | 10.00% | 🟢 |

| Efficiency Ratios | Value | Target | Result |
|---|---|---|---|
| Return On Equity | 54.03% | 30.00% | 🟢 |
| Return On Total Assets | 26.56% | 25.00% | 🟢 |
| Return On Capital Employed | 30.78% | 25.00% | 🟢 |
| ECROCE | 30.84% | 20.00% | 🟢 |

| Asset Usage | Value | Target | Result |
|---|---|---|---|
| Activity Ratio | 2.05 times | 2.50 times | 🔴 |
| Asset Turnover Ratio | 1.77 times | 2.00 times | 🔴 |
| GM Return on Inventory | 1,159.48% | 1,000.00% | 🟢 |
| Working Capital Absorption Rate | 6.19% | 35.00% | 🟢 |

| Gearing | Value | Target | Result |
|---|---|---|---|
| Interest Coverage Ratio | 117.55 times | 3.00 times | 🟢 |
| Debt to Equity Ratio | 0.78:1 | 1.00:1 | 🟢 |

| Other | Value | Target | Result |
|---|---|---|---|
| Sustainable Growth Rate | 18.05% | 10.00% | 🟢 |
| Marginal Cash | 42.70% | 0.00% | 🟢 |
| Earnings per Share | $10,128.86 | $0 | 🟢 |
| Free Cash Flow | $968,022.50 | $0 | 🟢 |

Capitaliz

## Breakeven Analysis

The breakeven analysis shows a strong focus on variable costs and a very strong safety margin which shows the business could drop sales by 30.70% and still be 'OK'.

FY 2021

# Breakeven Analysis

| | |
|---|---|
| Total Revenue $8,093,000 | |
| Variable Costs $4,136,022 | |
| Fixed Costs $2,742,182 | |
| Breakeven $5,608,441 | |
| Safety Margin 30.70% | |

| Variable costs | | Fixed costs | |
|---|---|---|---|
| COS Goods | $0 | COS Fixed | $0 |
| COS Other | $4,101,720 | Non-Cash | $0 |
| Variable Expenses | $34,302 | Fixed Expenses | $2,742,182 |
| | | Non-Cash Expenses | $0 |
| TOTAL Variable Costs | $4,136,022 | TOTAL Fixed Costs | $2,742,182 |

| | |
|---|---|
| Total Sales | $8,093,000 |
| Variable Cost % | 51.11% |
| Breakeven | $5,608,441 |
| Safety Margin | 30.70% |

Capitaliz

## Revenue to Cash Analysis

FY 2021

# Revenue to Cash Analysis

| | | |
|---|---|---:|
| Revenue | | $8,093,000 |
| Change in Receivables | add | $257,162 |
| Cash from Sales | | $8,350,162 |
| | | |
| Cost of Sales | | $4,101,720 |
| Change in Inventory | less | $4,841 |
| Change in Payables | add | $49,317 |
| Cash cost of Production | | $4,146,196 |
| | | |
| Cash Gross Profit | | $4,203,966 |
| | | |
| Variable Expenses | less | $34,302 |
| Fixed Expenses | less | $2,742,182 |
| Other Income | add | $0 |
| Operating Cash Profit Before tax | | $1,427,482 |
| | | |
| Cash Tax Paid (notional) | less | $0 |
| Changes in Tax Payable | add | $9,276 |
| Operating Cash Profit After Tax | | $1,436,758 |
| | | |
| Interest | less | $10,334 |
| Changes to Dividends Paid | less | $346,501 |
| Normalised Cash Profit | | $1,079,923 |

Capitali**z**

Free Cash Flow

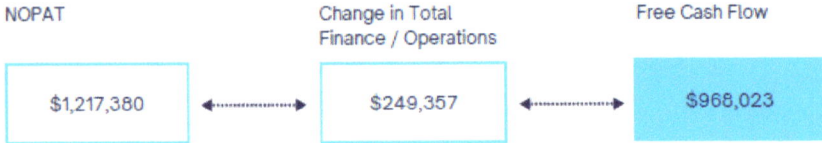

FY 2021

# Free Cash Flow

| NOPAT | Change in Total Finance / Operations | Free Cash Flow |
|---|---|---|
| $1,217,380 | $249,357 | $968,023 |

| Change in Total Operations | Opening | Closing | | Change |
|---|---|---|---|---|
| Accounts Receivable | $922,340 | $665,178 | ▼ | -$257,162 |
| Inventory | $346,651 | $341,810 | ▼ | -$4,841 |
| Other Current Assets (excl. cash) | $193,648 | $584,296 | ▲ | $390,648 |
| Accounts Payable | $555,009 | $505,692 | ▼ | -$49,317 |
| Tax Liability | $27,311 | $36,587 | ▲ | $9,276 |
| Other Current Liabilities | $53,180 | $84,357 | ▲ | $31,177 |
| Fixed Assets | $2,447,714 | $2,545,600 | ▲ | $97,886 |
| Other non-current assets | $208,446 | $222,408 | ▲ | $13,962 |
| Investments | $0 | $0 | | $0 |
| Total Operations | $3,483,299 | $3,732,656 | ▲ | $249,357 |

■ Positive Effect on Free Cash Flow       ■ Negative Effect on Free Cash Flow

Capitaliz

It All Begins with Insights | Capitaliz

51

## Sustainable Growth

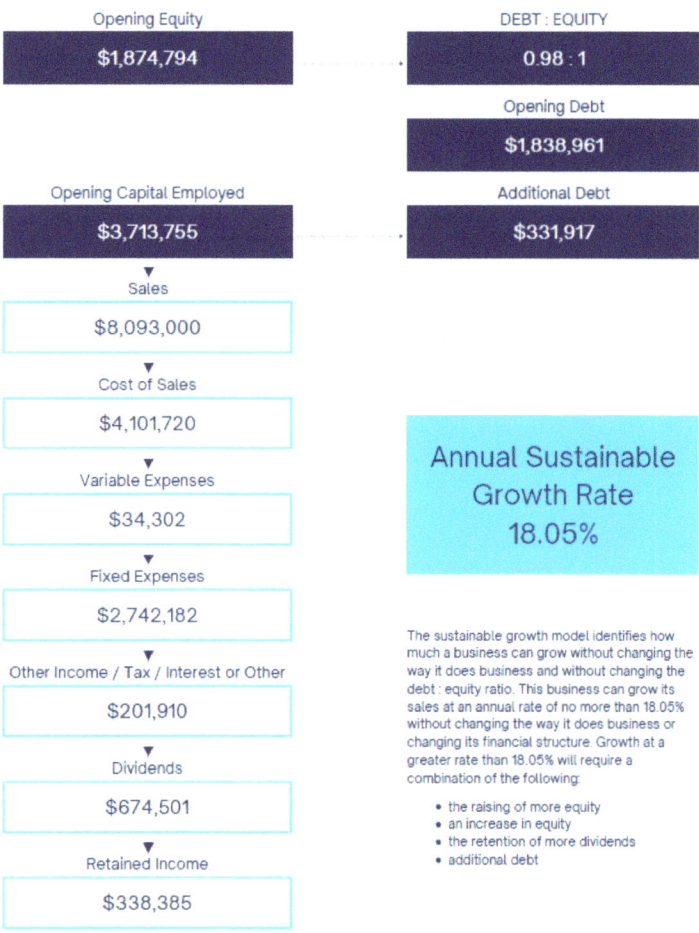

The sustainable growth rate shows ability to grow the business at approximately 18.05% which is a reasonable result. This is used to highlight the growth factors which exist and the ability for the business to fund this growth.

The sustainable growth rate is a useful tool providing valuable insights to establish the funding position moving forward, especially if a part of the strategy is to grow the business.

FY 2021

# Sustainable Growth

| Opening Equity | DEBT : EQUITY |
|---|---|
| $1,874,794 | 0.98 : 1 |

| | Opening Debt |
|---|---|
| | $1,838,961 |

| Opening Capital Employed | Additional Debt |
|---|---|
| $3,713,755 | $331,917 |

**Sales**
$8,093,000

**Cost of Sales**
$4,101,720

**Variable Expenses**
$34,302

**Fixed Expenses**
$2,742,182

**Other Income / Tax / Interest or Other**
$201,910

**Dividends**
$674,501

**Retained Income**
$338,385

### Annual Sustainable Growth Rate
### 18.05%

The sustainable growth model identifies how much a business can grow without changing the way it does business and without changing the debt : equity ratio. This business can grow its sales at an annual rate of no more than 18.05% without changing the way it does business or changing its financial structure. Growth at a greater rate than 18.05% will require a combination of the following:

- the raising of more equity
- an increase in equity
- the retention of more dividends
- additional debt

## Credit Risk Scorecards

FY 2021

# Credit Risk Scorecard

A+

**Primary Exit**  2 out of 2
- Debt Payback (yrs)
- Interest Times Cover

**Secondary Exit**  3 out of 3
- Debt to Equity Ratio
- Debt to Total Assets
- Estimated Recoverable Value

**Debt Servicing**  3 out of 3
- Debt Facilities / EBITDA
- Debt Service Cover
- Notional Debt Service (yrs)

## Benchmarking Analysis

The benchmarking highlights over and under performance of business against industry peers and similar industries/businesses.

FY 2021

# Benchmarking Firms

| Cost Structure Benchmarks | Smith Engineering (2021) | IBISWorld (Engineering Consulting) |
|---|---|---|
| **Revenue** | **$8,093,000** | **-** |
| Revenue | 100.0% | 100.0% |
| Cost of Sales * | 49.7% | 47.2% |
| **Gross Margin** | **50.3%** | **52.9%** |
| Occupancy costs | 1.4% | 1.6% |
| Depreciation | 3.2% | 2.1% |
| Repairs & maintenance | 0.9% | 0.4% |
| Total employment costs | 21.1% | 25.0% |
| All other costs | 8.7% | 9.8% |
| Total expenses | 35.3% | 38.9% |
| **Profit Margin (before tax)** | **15.0%** | **14.0%** |

Capitaliz

Employment costs in Smith Engineering are 21.1%, which is lower than the average of 25% for similar sized businesses.

## Profit Gap Analysis

The profit gap analysis shows several areas of real cost savings in both wages and salaries and asset turnover. Combining these improves profitability by over $265,000.

FY 2021

# Profit Gap Analysis

### Your Profit Gaps Relative to the Most Profitable Firms

| | The Business | Benchmark Firms | Profit Gap |
|---|---|---|---|
| Average benchmark COGS | | 47.15% | |
| Your business revenue | $8,093,000 | | |
| COGS benchmark | | $3,815,850 | |
| Your COGS | $4,019,686 | | |
| % of Revenue | 49.67% | | |
| Profit Gap | | | $203,837 |
| Average benchmark Employment costs | | 25.00% | |
| Your business revenue | $8,093,000 | | |
| Employment costs benchmark | | $2,023,250 | No Profit Gap |
| Your Employment costs | $1,706,907 | | |
| % of Revenue | 21.09% | | |
| Profit Gap | | | |
| Average benchmark Overhead costs | | 13.90% | |
| Your business revenue | $8,093,000 | | |
| Overhead costs benchmark | | $1,124,927 | No Profit Gap |
| Your Overhead costs | $1,044,254 | | |
| % of Revenue | 12.90% | | |
| Profit Gap | | | |

### Your Total Profit Gap

| | Relative to Benchmark Firms |
|---|---|
| Reducing your cost of sales purchases could yield | $203,837 |
| Bringing your personnel numbers back could yield | - |
| Reducing non-wages & salary overheads could yield | - |
| **Total Profit Gap** | **$265,935** |
| Which equates to the following % of your current Profit | 21.89% |

## Foundation and Weighted Average Cost of Capital (WACC)

Interestingly, it is quite common to see businesses which perform well financially score poorly in the non-financial and exit readiness aspects of the business.

The quality of the non-financial aspects of the business impacts on the risk in the business and ultimately the weighted average cost of capital (WACC). This in turn, impacts the valuation itself. Many business owners are not aware of this impact and simply focus on profit alone.

FY 2021

# Foundation Scorecard

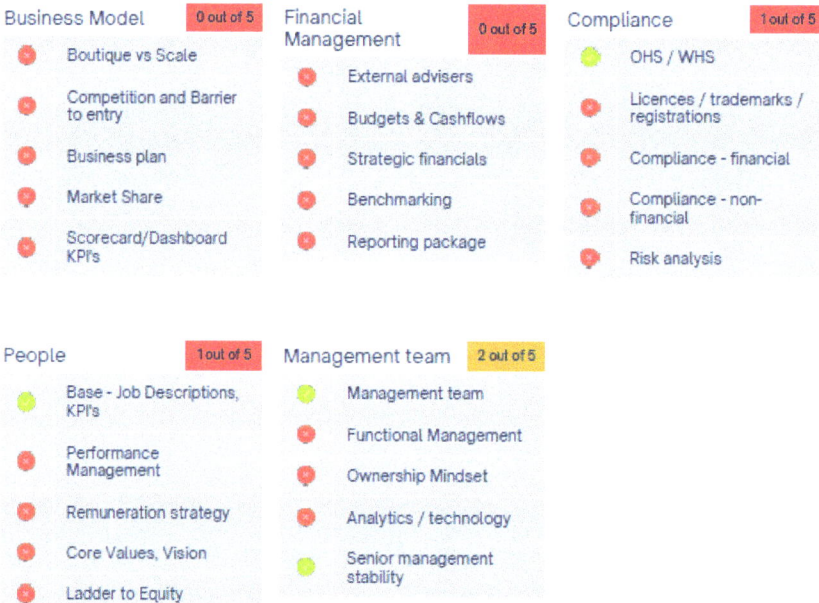

E+

**Business Model** — 0 out of 5
- Boutique vs Scale
- Competition and Barrier to entry
- Business plan
- Market Share
- Scorecard/Dashboard KPI's

**Financial Management** — 0 out of 5
- External advisers
- Budgets & Cashflows
- Strategic financials
- Benchmarking
- Reporting package

**Compliance** — 1 out of 5
- OHS / WHS
- Licences / trademarks / registrations
- Compliance - financial
- Compliance - non-financial
- Risk analysis

**People** — 1 out of 5
- Base - Job Descriptions, KPI's
- Performance Management
- Remuneration strategy
- Core Values, Vision
- Ladder to Equity

**Management team** — 2 out of 5
- Management team
- Functional Management
- Ownership Mindset
- Analytics / technology
- Senior management stability

Capitaliz

## Strategic Growth

In addition to the non-financial risk/operations assessment, we need to review the business through the "lens" of a potential buyer:

1. Will they find it attractive?
2. What are the key features they are looking for?
3. Is the business currently sale or exit ready?

We will now consider each of the components of the strategic growth scorecard from a buyer's perspective.

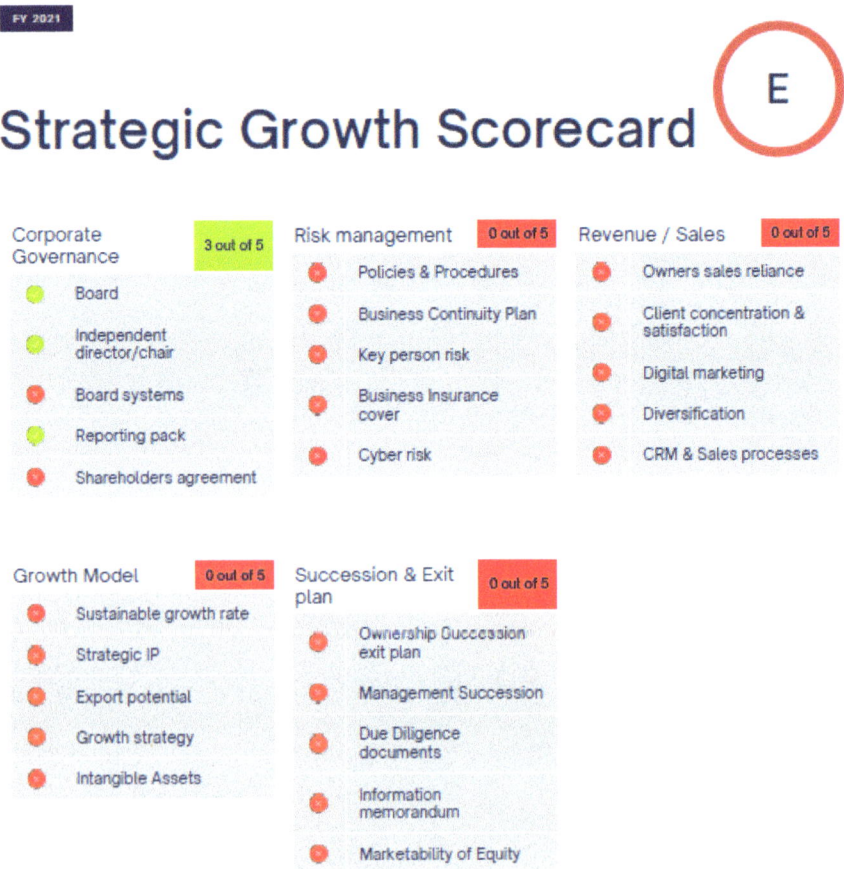

FY 2021

# Strategic Growth Scorecard  E

| Corporate Governance | 3 out of 5 |
|---|---|
| Board | |
| Independent director/chair | |
| Board systems | |
| Reporting pack | |
| Shareholders agreement | |

| Risk management | 0 out of 5 |
|---|---|
| Policies & Procedures | |
| Business Continuity Plan | |
| Key person risk | |
| Business Insurance cover | |
| Cyber risk | |

| Revenue / Sales | 0 out of 5 |
|---|---|
| Owners sales reliance | |
| Client concentration & satisfaction | |
| Digital marketing | |
| Diversification | |
| CRM & Sales processes | |

| Growth Model | 0 out of 5 |
|---|---|
| Sustainable growth rate | |
| Strategic IP | |
| Export potential | |
| Growth strategy | |
| Intangible Assets | |

| Succession & Exit plan | 0 out of 5 |
|---|---|
| Ownership Succession exit plan | |
| Management Succession | |
| Due Diligence documents | |
| Information memorandum | |
| Marketability of Equity | |

Page - 34

Capitaliz

# Non-financial Commentary

When assessing the valuation of any business, there are some foundational items that buyers, investors, and lenders would expect to see in a mid-market company. The foundation scorecard measures these essential items and assesses the overall risk score of the business based on the results.

*Business Model*

## Boutique vs Scale

All businesses sit along the scale of boutique (think Ferrari) and scale (think Toyota). If you want to maximize the value of your business and exit successfully, then your business model needs to be either boutique or scale, and every part of the business needs to match this model. If it's a mix of both, you're in 'no man's land', and your ability to maximize business value decreases substantially.

## Competition and Barrier to Entry

Competition exists in nearly any industry and for every business, but not all competition is equal. The Barrier to entry (for example, licenses and qualifications the owner might need before they can operate the business or a register of expensive machinery and equipment required to commence business) can create a level of protection from the competition - some businesses (think real estate agents) for example, are highly competitive. As a general rule, the harder it is for new entrants to challenge incumbents, the better.

## Business Plan

As the saying goes, if you fail to plan, you plan to fail. The purpose of the Strategic Business Plan is not only to illustrate the feasibility of your business idea but also to serve as a communication document to your key stakeholders, investors, and employees. The plan should map critical milestones, risks, and opportunities for value acceleration.

## Market Share

There are advantages and disadvantages to controlling more significant percentages of a business's market, but monitoring that level over time provides management with a powerful instrument in guiding the business's strategy in the long term. For example, firms with a substantial market share are often less susceptible to pricing competition.

### Scorecard/Dashboard KPIs

Knowledge is power. Technology has advanced to a point where businesses can monitor, in near-real-time, the performance of critical activities their companies undertake (pipeline, HR, financial metrics and CRM.) While this was once the realm of the best performing businesses, adopting these technological and data-driven approaches to daily decision-making is critical to business performance.

## *Financial Management*

### External Advisors

External advisors are an excellent source of new ideas. They can provide an outsider's perspective on issues that may be difficult to resolve internally and add specific experience and expertise that business owners cannot hold.

### Budgets & Cashflows

The business direction will likely suffer if adequate tools are not in place to illustrate its financial position and where it expects and aims to be in the future. Projecting budgets and cashflows will guide performance, and a review of actual performance vs these goals holds stakeholders accountable for performance.

### Strategic Financials

Long-term strategic forecasts are a critical ingredient in long-term strategic planning. The strategic financial goals must match the business's long-term (exit) plan.

### Benchmarking

Benchmarking can be a helpful exercise in determining the business' competitiveness and can be used to inform or support the objectives set out in the Strategic Business Plan. Comparison with competitors and industry averages can highlight over or underperformance.

### Reporting Package

A monthly reporting pack should include everything the board or leadership team needs to make informed decisions. It should contain a mixture of financial, non-financial and leading KPIs to measure and monitor business performance to match the business and financial plans.

## *People*

### Base – Job Descriptions, KPIs

A position description is valuable for communicating objectives and roles to staff. Great position descriptions stimulate employee engagement and should clearly describe roles, responsibilities, and KPIs.

## Performance Management

Performance reviews are an opportunity to align your employees' interests with the goals and objectives of the business. Many businesses overlook formal performance reviews and informal performance feedback to increase employee engagement and monitor performance.

## Remuneration Strategy

A remuneration strategy that aligns reward with crucial business outcomes will encourage performance and produce a close alignment between behavioral results and business outcomes.

## Core Values, Vision

If your business is clear on its values – why it is in business and how it wants to behave worldwide - customers, employees, and suppliers are much more likely to be aligned. Alignment is critical to business success.

## Ladder to Equity

There is a sequential order in which to use remuneration to bring out the best in a business's talent. In an ideal world, an employee would graduate up the ladder sequentially, beginning with income (e.g., a base salary), then Income (e.g., a commission structure), then a profit share, then equity (or partial ownership itself) and lastly, control (e.g., directorship).

## *Management Team*

## Management Team

Leadership is doing the right things; management is doing things right. Your company will have a much better chance of success if your managers work well together, with clear roles and productive meetings and can run the business without owner involvement.

## Functional Management

Organizing roles and functions around a central managerial philosophy creates rhythm in a business, keeping role overlap, duplication, confusion and gaps to a minimum.

## Ownership Mindset

The very best businesses communicate information about financial performance to their staff in a responsible manner, so they know how their day-to-day actions impact it, but also supply them with a structure that enables those same staff to influence the performance of the business positively. Ownership mindset is about employees thinking and acting like business owners.

## Analytics/Technology
The businesses best positioned to take advantage of rapidly changing conditions are those with a strong command of internal and external data and can use it to make decisions. This should occur in every area of operation within the business.

## Senior Management Stability
Longevity of tenure among managerial staff is a classic hallmark of a well-run business. A senior experienced team who has been with the business for an extended period will drive culture and performance.

### *Risk Management*

## Policies & Procedures
Policies and procedures are especially useful as risk alleviation tools. For example, if a key person with unique knowledge leaves your business, you may have difficulty continuing operations until that person is replaced. With appropriate documentation in place knowledge can be transferred to others and enable staff training.

## IT Systems/BCP
Emergencies and natural disasters can cripple a business. With appropriate forethought, the risk can be alleviated.

## Key Person Risk
Reducing key person risk is critical to increasing a company's value. Insurance can help to mitigate risk, but only if it is considered and implemented before a key person becomes unavailable, rather than after.

## Shareholder Agreement
Some businesses are thrown into chaos by the death or incapacity of an owner. While reducing dependence on owners is an excellent start, there should also be a plan in place for ownership transfer, to reduce disruption.

## Business Cover
Insurance is top of mind for most people when they think about risk management. Each business has unique insurance needs which change over time as the business changes. Involving knowledgeable advisors who know your business in regular review processes is great practice in managing risk.

## Beta Factor Assessment

The following tool simply allows us to accurately assess various risks that impact the business and its value. Risk is a significant aspect of the valuation equation.

**FY 2021**

# Beta Factor Scorecards

### Economy

| | Lower Risk -0.5 | 0 | Higher Risk +0.5 | |
|---|---|---|---|---|
| Foreign Exchange Impacts | | | | 0.1 |
| Interest Rates | | | | 0 |
| Inflation | | | | 0 |

### Industry

| | Lower Risk -0.5 | 0 | Higher Risk +0.5 | |
|---|---|---|---|---|
| Future Impacts | | | | 0.2 |
| Type of Business | | | | 0.1 |
| Product Mix | | | | 0.2 |
| Competition | | | | 0.2 |
| Barrier to Entry | | | | 0.2 |
| Market Share | | | | 0 |
| Specialised Asset | | | | 0.2 |
| Marketability of Equity | | | | 0.4 |

### Business

| | Lower Risk -0.5 | 0 | Higher Risk +0.5 | |
|---|---|---|---|---|
| Location | | | | 0.1 |
| Mgmt. Skills / Performance Record | | | | 0.2 |
| Past Performance - Sustainability | | | | 0 |
| Intellectual Property | | | | 0 |
| Technology | | | | 0 |
| Marketability of Ownership | | | | 0.4 |
| Business Risk (non-financial) | | | | 0.3 |

### Market Leveraging

| Average Market Leveraging | Market Asset Beta | Net Adjustment | Asset Beta |
|---|---|---|---|
| 40.00% | 0.70 | 2.60 | 3.30 |

Capitaliz

# Risk Factors

| Risk factor | What this risk factor is about | Suggested improvement strategies |
|---|---|---|
| **Economy** | | |
| Foreign Exchange | The extent to which changes in FX rates impact on business volume | Customers of Smith Engineering are all domiciled in Australia, but occasionally some components are imported, and the cost of those items are therefore exposed to currency fluctuations. We have reflected this as a minor risk. |
| Interest rates | Whether changes in interest rates impact on volume of business carried out | Businesses that are vulnerable to this risk tend to have enduring or growing levels of debt. Smith Engineering is showing a track record of debt reduction and is therefore rated at an average level of risk. No strategic recommendations to make beyond continued debt reduction where commercially astute. |
| Inflation | The extent to which the business is vulnerable to changes in the rate of inflation | Businesses most exposed to inflation risk are businesses with low elasticity of demand and low margins. Smith Engineering is neither. We therefore rate it as risk neutral and make no further recommendations around this. |
| **Industry** | | |
| Future impacts | Whether the business is vulnerable than the market average when exposed to future business impact (disruption) | Our view is that Smith Engineering is less vulnerable than the market average to future business impact, however, we apply a general level of risk to all private businesses owing to a pattern of disruption. |
| Type of Business | Whether the type of business makes it risky than the market | Our view is that Smith Engineering does not have an abnormal level of risk here. While engineering services and associated services are often legally mandatory, they are tied to the general level of confidence and overall economic output of the market. It is also our understanding that a program |

| Risk factor | What this risk factor is about | Suggested improvement strategies |
|---|---|---|
| | | of industry/ sectoral diversification has been undertaken in recent years, which we believe to be a sound approach to management of risk in this area. No further recommendations. |
| Product Mix | Range and scope of product and the likelihood it will satisfy market demand and the customer's value proposition | Our understanding is that Smith Engineering's product offering is under review and has a normal level of risk exposure with respect to the broader industry sector. No further recommendations here. |
| Competition | How powerful the competition is | Our understanding is that Smith Engineering's competitors pose a normal level of risk compared to other businesses of its size. However, this sector is maturing and exposed to disruption, so we have included some moderate risk weighting. |
| Barrier to Entry | The extent to which the business is dependent on IP and its ability to protect IP, such as patents etc. | Our understanding is that there are no special legal requirements to conduct an engineering services business. While Smith Engineering has a very high concentration of talent and an enduring brand, there aren't major monetary obstacles, such as purchase of equipment or trade licenses to prevent competition from entering the market. This is an intrinsic risk to this business. |
| Market Share | Relates to the business' market share and concentration of individual market revenue to the business' total revenue | Our understanding is that Smith Engineering has enjoyed a significant and stable portion of the market for many years. |
| Specialized Asset | Refers to the extent to which there are a significant level of physical assets that are difficult to remove or relocate | There are several physical assets of this nature, but the risk is somewhat mitigated by some existing contingency plans in place. We would encourage a review of these plans and updates where necessary. |

| Risk factor | What this risk factor is about | Suggested improvement strategies |
|---|---|---|
| Marketability of Equity | How readily marketable is the equity in the business relative to the average. Actively traded listed companies are the most liquid, unlisted companies are the least liquid and thinly traded listed companies are somewhere in between. | Equity in privately held business assets is high risk. The equity ownership is difficult to value and difficult to transact. Partial sales of equity even more so. Nevertheless, businesses like Smith Engineering should work with professionals to ensure the business is attractive as possible to would-be purchasers or investors. |
| **Business** | | |
| Location | Relative risk to physical location (distance from key suppliers, ports, customers, etc.)<br><br>Diversity of location exposure to local economy | We believe Smith Engineering has a somewhat higher level of risk than other businesses of its size (in other service industries) in that revenue is concentrated in NSW and resourcing in particular in Newcastle. Other offices are being developed, and we encourage this to continue to lower this risk. The possibility of joint ventures elsewhere might also be explored. |
| Management skills/ performance record | How does management's past performance compare with that of average? (Skillset, execution - strategic, financial, operational, commercial, and technical) | Smith Engineering will need to develop and sustain a culture of deep commitment to corporate governance. |
| Past performance - Sustainability | How volatile has the past operational and financial performance relative to the market average | Compounded annual rate of revenue growth from 2018 - 2021 was 6.6%. We recommend increasing the robustness of the financial and non-financial reporting rigor with a special emphasis on dashboard familiarity throughout the business. Moreover, we recommend investing in a new ERP system to make the necessary information flows more reliable and to reduce risk of information opacity among key decision makers. |

| Risk factor | What this risk factor is about | Suggested improvement strategies |
|---|---|---|
| Intellectual Property | The extent to which the business is dependent on IP and its ability to protect IP, such as patents etc. | Our understanding is that Smith Engineering is not reliant on proprietary Intellectual Property. We therefore rate it as risk neutral and make no further recommendations in this area. |
| Technology | Refers to the extent to which the business is vulnerable to technology developments | Our understanding is that the business has a normal level of vulnerability to technology developments consistent with service businesses generally. |
| Marketability of Ownership | This relates to the difficulty in both valuing and transacting small privately held business assets. | Privately owned businesses are not listed securities, they are therefore difficult to price and illiquid assets. We therefore include some risk in our calculation to reflect this. |
| Business risk (non-financial) | This risk is directly related to overall non-financial scorecard result and represents total other risk in the business. | N/A |

## Weighted Average Cost of Capital (WACC)

This calculation is also important to the overall result. The WACC allows us to determine the cost of capital and importantly what return we should be generating given the risk/s involved.

FY 2021

# Weighted Average Cost of Capital (WACC)

### Cost of Debt

| | |
|---|---|
| Marginal Interest Rate | 4.89% |
| Marginal Corporate Tax Rate | 26.00% |
| Cost of Borrowing Funds | 3.62% |

### Cost of Equity

| | |
|---|---|
| Risk Free Rate of Return | 1.70% |
| Market Risk Premium | 6.00% |
| Asset Beta | 3.30 |
| Market Value Debt | 43.50% |
| Leveraged Beta | 5.18 |
| Cost of Equity Funds | 32.78% |

### Weighted Average Cost of Capital

| Before-Tax WACC | After-Tax WACC |
|---|---|
| 27.16% | 20.10% |

## Profitability Analysis

FY 2021

# Economic Profit Analysis

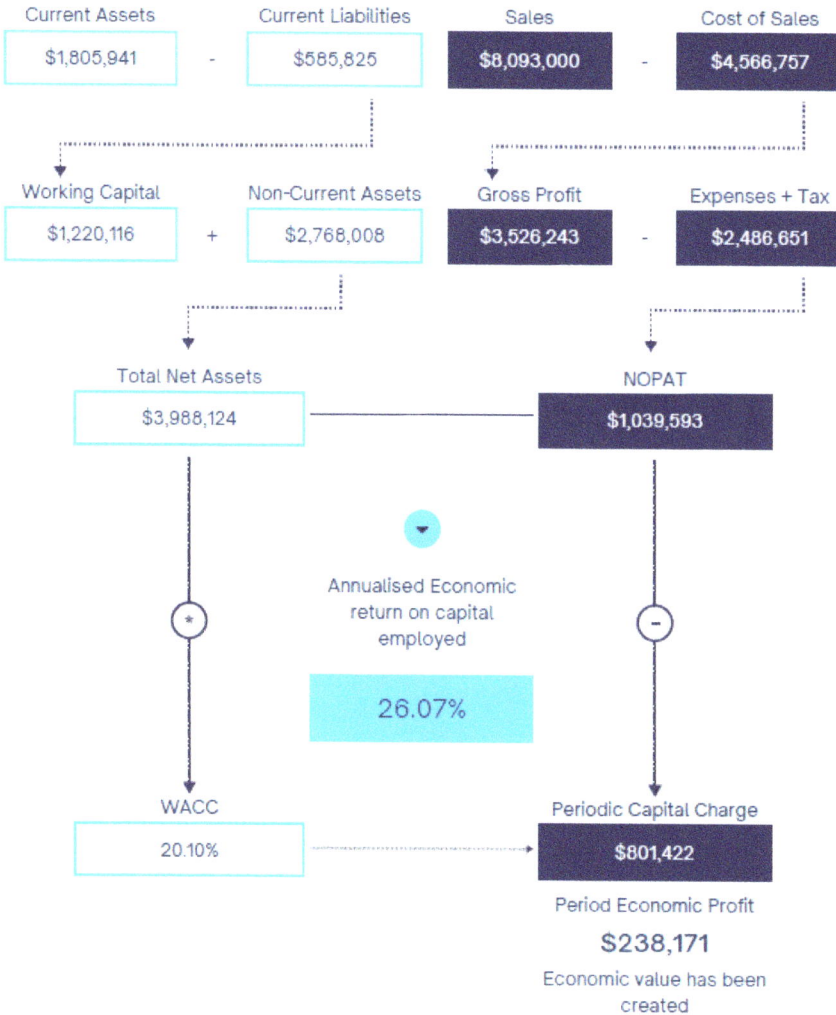

| Current Assets | | Current Liabilities | | Sales | | Cost of Sales |
|---|---|---|---|---|---|---|
| $1,805,941 | - | $585,825 | | $8,093,000 | - | $4,566,757 |

| Working Capital | | Non-Current Assets | | Gross Profit | | Expenses + Tax |
|---|---|---|---|---|---|---|
| $1,220,116 | + | $2,768,008 | | $3,526,243 | - | $2,486,651 |

| Total Net Assets | NOPAT |
|---|---|
| $3,988,124 | $1,039,593 |

Annualised Economic return on capital employed

**26.07%**

| WACC | Periodic Capital Charge |
|---|---|
| 20.10% | $801,422 |

Period Economic Profit

**$238,171**

Economic value has been created

Capitaliz

## Enterprise Valuation

FY 2021

# Business Valuation

| | 2018 | 2019 | 2020 | 2021 | 2022 Forecast | |
|---|---|---|---|---|---|---|
| Revenue | $5,771,884 | $6,561,310 | $7,481,200 | $8,093,000 | | |
| EBIT | $692,255 | $1,169,957 | $707,311 | $1,322,153 | | |
| Op Tax | $125,505 | $247,094 | $127,666 | $282,560 | | |
| NOPAT | $566,750 | $922,863 | $579,645 | $1,039,593 | $1,060,385 | |
| Growth Rate | | 63% | -37% | 79% | 2% | |
| Weighting | | 10.00% | 20.00% | 40.00% | 30.00% | |
| Weighted Average of Earnings | | | | | | $942,168 |

## Enterprise Valuation

| | |
|---|---|
| Cost of Capital | 20.10% |
| Growth Rate | 2.00% |
| Capitalisation Multiple (intrinsic) | 5.64 |
| Enterprise Value (Capitalisation of Earnings Method) | $5,309,454 |

Capitaliz

Equity Valuation

FY 2021

# Business Valuation

## Equity Valuation

| | |
|---|---|
| Enterprise Value (Capitalisation of Earnings Method) | $5,309,454 |
| Add: Cash & Cash Equivalents | $214,657 |
| Add: Financial Assets | $0 |
| Add: Non-operating Assets (land & buildings, vacant land) | $0 |
| Add: Loans to directors / related parties | $584,300 |
| Add: Other Surplus Assets (artworks, personal use assets (cars, etc.)) | $0 |
| | |
| Less: Short-term Debt | $107,000 |
| Less: Long-term Debt | $1,627,135 |
| Less: Loans from Directors / Related Parties | $0 |
| Equity Value (Capitalisation of Earnings Method) | $4,374,276 |
| Number of Shares Issued | 100 |
| Owner's Value per Share | $43,742.76 |

Capitaliz

## Forecast Profit and Value Potential

FY 2021

# Value Potential

| | As of today | Resolve profit gap | Best in Class financials | Attractiveness | Strategic Exit |
|---|---|---|---|---|---|
| Revenue | $8,093,000 | $8,093,000 | $8,093,000 | $8,093,000 | $8,093,000 |
| EBITDA | $1,576,713 | $1,851,748 | $1,873,160 | $1,873,160 | $1,873,160 |
| NOPAT | $1,039,593 | $1,255,849 | $1,272,685 | $1,272,685 | $1,272,685 |
| EBITDA Multiple | 3.37 | 3.37 | 3.37 | 4.15 | 4.83 |
| NOPAT Multiple | 5.11 | 5.11 | 5.11 | 6.11 | 7.11 |
| Valuation | $5.31M | $6.41M | $6.50M | $7.78M | $9.05M |

Legend: Current valuation — Potential Valuation

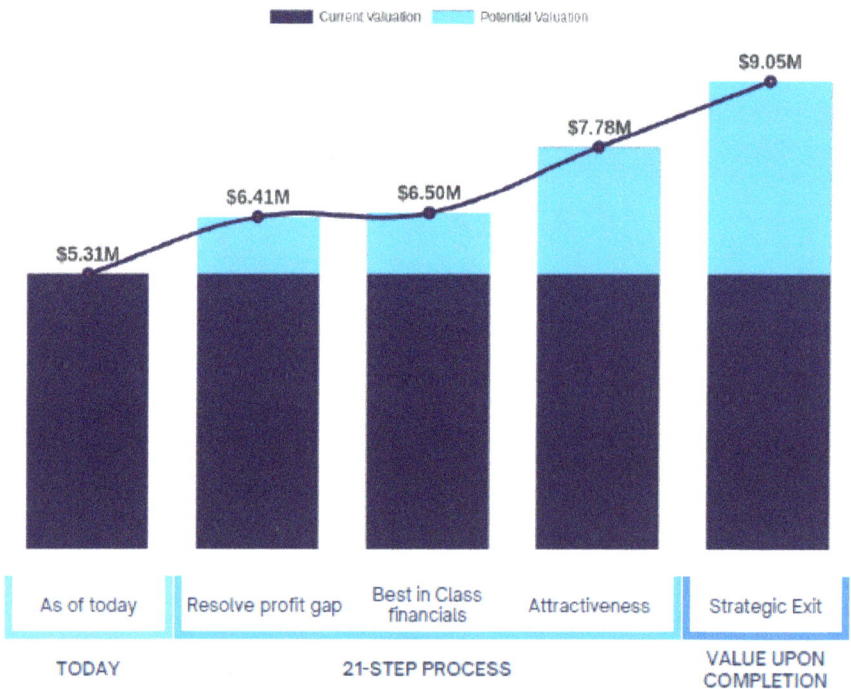

$9.05M

$7.78M

$6.41M    $6.50M

$5.31M

| As of today | Resolve profit gap | Best in Class financials | Attractiveness | Strategic Exit |

TODAY          21-STEP PROCESS          VALUE UPON COMPLETION

Capitaliz

## VPI™ – Value Potential Index

The VPI will become the industry standard for measuring value and determining SME value potential over time. Our proprietary index is based on over 800 business valuations over 12 years where we can track the key metrics that drive valuations and project potential value over time, based upon implementing the recommendations from our Capitaliz Business Insights Report.

The index includes economic, industry and business-based risk scores to determine the appropriate multiple and the gaps identified in the report for profit gap, benchmarking, exit readiness and attractiveness to determine the value potential. The index is recalculated each time a new valuation is completed and updated regularly with any changes in economic factors, industry trends or business sentiment.

Use of our proprietary index allows us to accurately assess value potential for each business and determine the most appropriate actions to take in order of priority that will most affect the valuation. Monthly use of Capitaliz to track actions and dynamically revalue the business each quarter (with updated financials) allows the process to be monitored and measured and all stakeholders to be held accountable for agreed actions.

Many businesses owners erroneously believe that financial performance improvement is the only means of increasing the value of the business. In fact, closing the profit gap and achieving best in class will lead to increased financial performance and therefore increase the value of the business. However, at the right-hand side of diagram, we observe areas of substantial potential value improvement also include the boosting of attractiveness to external buyers and careful selection of a strategic acquirer, which have only an indirect relationship with profitability.

We can see the potential value uplift for Smith Engineering Pty Ltd, could be in the order $3.74 million over today's value, if recommendations in this report are carried out successfully.

22% of that improvement would come from closing the profit gap and reaching best practice profit margins. 70% of value improvement would be due to improving attractiveness and strategic acquirer selection.

## 21-Step Implementation Plan

After a detailed review of the report, the goal setting analysis and discussion of the proposed implementation plan, the owners agreed to proceed with a strategic advisory engagement as outlined by the implementation plan.

# Capitaliz - Implementation Roadmap
## Smith Engineering

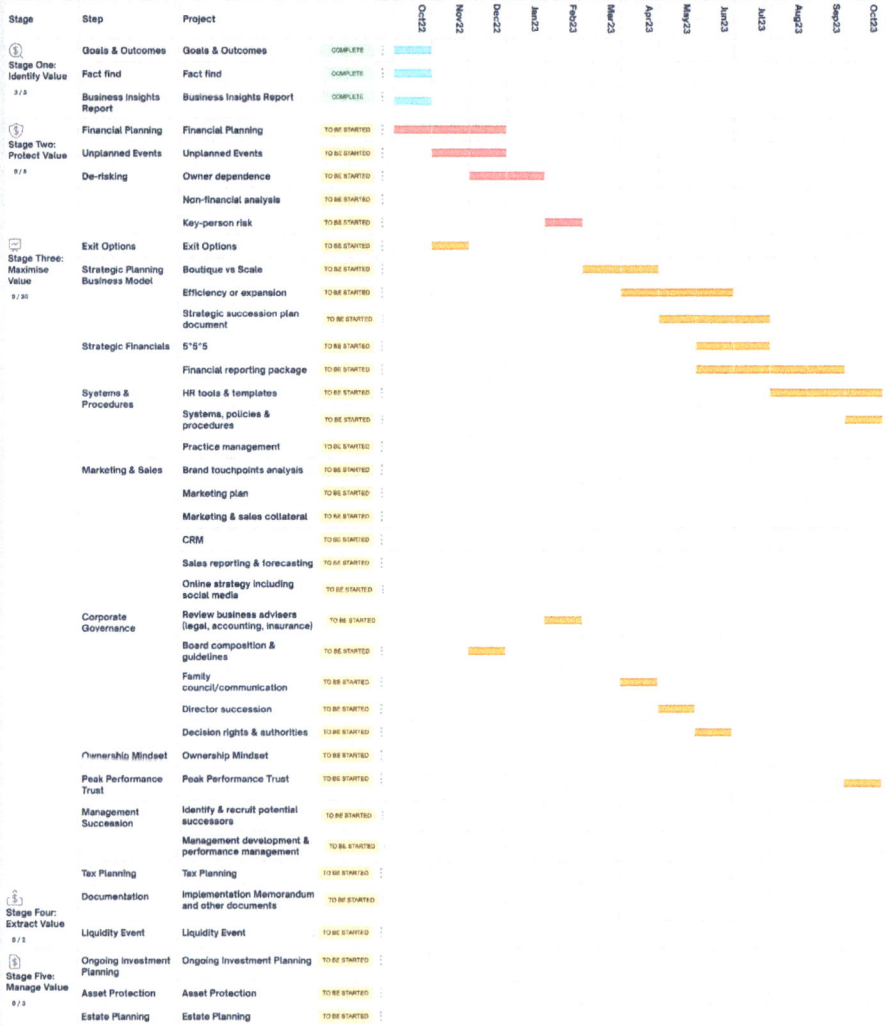

| Stage | Step | Project | Status | Oct22 | Nov22 | Dec22 | Jan23 | Feb23 | Mar23 | Apr23 | May23 | Jun23 | Jul23 | Aug23 | Sep23 | Oct23 |
|---|---|---|---|---|---|---|---|---|---|---|---|---|---|---|---|---|
| **Stage One: Identify Value** 3/3 | Goals & Outcomes | Goals & Outcomes | COMPLETE | | | | | | | | | | | | | |
| | Fact find | Fact find | COMPLETE | | | | | | | | | | | | | |
| | Business Insights Report | Business Insights Report | COMPLETE | | | | | | | | | | | | | |
| **Stage Two: Protect Value** 0/5 | Financial Planning | Financial Planning | TO BE STARTED | | | | | | | | | | | | | |
| | Unplanned Events | Unplanned Events | TO BE STARTED | | | | | | | | | | | | | |
| | De-risking | Owner dependence | TO BE STARTED | | | | | | | | | | | | | |
| | | Non-financial analysis | TO BE STARTED | | | | | | | | | | | | | |
| | | Key-person risk | TO BE STARTED | | | | | | | | | | | | | |
| **Stage Three: Maximise Value** 0/30 | Exit Options | Exit Options | TO BE STARTED | | | | | | | | | | | | | |
| | Strategic Planning Business Model | Boutique vs Scale | TO BE STARTED | | | | | | | | | | | | | |
| | | Efficiency or expansion | TO BE STARTED | | | | | | | | | | | | | |
| | | Strategic succession plan document | TO BE STARTED | | | | | | | | | | | | | |
| | Strategic Financials | 5*5*5 | TO BE STARTED | | | | | | | | | | | | | |
| | | Financial reporting package | TO BE STARTED | | | | | | | | | | | | | |
| | Systems & Procedures | HR tools & templates | TO BE STARTED | | | | | | | | | | | | | |
| | | Systems, policies & procedures | TO BE STARTED | | | | | | | | | | | | | |
| | | Practice management | TO BE STARTED | | | | | | | | | | | | | |
| | Marketing & Sales | Brand touchpoints analysis | TO BE STARTED | | | | | | | | | | | | | |
| | | Marketing plan | TO BE STARTED | | | | | | | | | | | | | |
| | | Marketing & sales collateral | TO BE STARTED | | | | | | | | | | | | | |
| | | CRM | TO BE STARTED | | | | | | | | | | | | | |
| | | Sales reporting & forecasting | TO BE STARTED | | | | | | | | | | | | | |
| | | Online strategy including social media | TO BE STARTED | | | | | | | | | | | | | |
| | Corporate Governance | Review business advisers (legal, accounting, insurance) | TO BE STARTED | | | | | | | | | | | | | |
| | | Board composition & guidelines | TO BE STARTED | | | | | | | | | | | | | |
| | | Family council/communication | TO BE STARTED | | | | | | | | | | | | | |
| | | Director succession | TO BE STARTED | | | | | | | | | | | | | |
| | | Decision rights & authorities | TO BE STARTED | | | | | | | | | | | | | |
| | Ownership Mindset | Ownership Mindset | TO BE STARTED | | | | | | | | | | | | | |
| | Peak Performance Trust | Peak Performance Trust | TO BE STARTED | | | | | | | | | | | | | |
| | Management Succession | Identify & recruit potential successors | TO BE STARTED | | | | | | | | | | | | | |
| | | Management development & performance management | TO BE STARTED | | | | | | | | | | | | | |
| | Tax Planning | Tax Planning | TO BE STARTED | | | | | | | | | | | | | |
| **Stage Four: Extract Value** 0/2 | Documentation | Implementation Memorandum and other documents | TO BE STARTED | | | | | | | | | | | | | |
| | Liquidity Event | Liquidity Event | TO BE STARTED | | | | | | | | | | | | | |
| **Stage Five: Manage Value** 0/3 | Ongoing Investment Planning | Ongoing Investment Planning | TO BE STARTED | | | | | | | | | | | | | |
| | Asset Protection | Asset Protection | TO BE STARTED | | | | | | | | | | | | | |
| | Estate Planning | Estate Planning | TO BE STARTED | | | | | | | | | | | | | |

## Client Advice

In the next stage of the process, the exit advisor will document an action plan to the business owner. This will outline the goals, summary of the key results and gaps that need to be addressed.

Next, this will be followed by a meeting to discuss the recommendations and ensure the client is on board with advice and confident that the goals set achieve the desired outcomes.

At this point of the process, now that the owners understand the value of the business today and, more importantly, the value potential into the future, they are keen to engage and embark on a journey to maximize value and achieve a successful exit. At Succession Plus, we do this by working with owners, and their advisors, over a 12 to 18-month period to work through our 21-step model over the five stages of value – identity, protect, maximize, extract, and manage.

The strategic advisory process is further outlined in ENJOY IT – our comprehensive guide to Business Succession and Exit Planning. Having worked with over 800 businesses over 12 years, the time, effort, and financial investment to maximize business value and achieve a successful exit can be a life-changing experience for business owners and their families. Our mission at Capitaliz is to help as many owners as possible to successfully navigate this journey.

# Why
# Capitaliz?

# Business Insights Report

- Industry leading assessment, valuation and roadmap tool for Business Succession and Exit Planning engagements.
- Used on over 800 clients over 13 years to identify value & value gap and map out the exit planning engagement.
- The platform allows efficient and accurate reports to allow "apples for apples" comparison across industries.
- The report uses 300 data points to automatically calculate company specific risk, beta and risk weightings and the business valuation.
- Dramatically improved conversion rate from Business Insights Report (trigger event) to advisory engagement.

# Value Potential

- Based on the Business Insights Report which uses over 150 non-financial data points for each client, our algorithm can quantify the value gap and identify key projects to accelerate business value – predicting the value potential for each client.
- Using the aggregated data across all businesses using the platform, we can accurately predict value potential by business, by industry, or by country.

# 21-Step Implementation Roadmap

- The platform uses the 21-step process which has been used for 10 years with business owners to identify, protect, accelerate, unlock, and manage value in privately owned businesses.
- The implementation roadmap is automatically generated by the platform and maps out an advisory engagement over 18 to 24 months.

# Dynamic Revaluation

- As the client progresses through the various projects identified by the report, the platform automatically calculates the valuation impact and updates the client dashboard.
- The platform clearly tracks the value gap and the value acceleration over time – highlighting the value of advice over the five stages of value.

## Collaborative Engagement

- Exit planning is by nature collaborative, requiring varied advisors to co-ordinate activities with owners to maximize value and achieve a successful exit.
- The Capitaliz platform allows multiple users to be added to projects and access the system – CPAs, attorneys, and others.
- The system allows internal collaboration, communication, and interaction, including multiple document formats.
- All interactions are date/time stamped for due diligence history.
- Management of tasks and notifications creates accountability for project activities across the entire team (internal and external).

Scan the QR code below or click here to find out more.

# It All Begins with Insights.

# Capitaliz
BY SUCCESSION+

www.ingramcontent.com/pod-product-compliance
Lightning Source LLC
Chambersburg PA
CBHW040908210326
41597CB00029B/5011